THE BUSINESSMAN'S WIFE

D1392592

BY THE SAME AUTHOR

Etiquette for the Businessman at Home and Abroad
Instant Business Letters
Personal Letters for Businessmen
Top Secretary
Creative Techniques for Management

THE BUSINESSMAN'S WIFE

Mary Bosticco

London

Mercury House Books Limited

First published 1972

© ISABEL LUCY MARY BOSTICCO, 1972

All rights reserved. Except for normal review purposes,
no part of this book may be reproduced
or utilised in any form or by any means,
electronic or mechanical, including photocopying,
recording or by any information storage
retrieval system, without permission of the publishers.

ISBN 0 220 66855 8

This book has been set in Intertype Baskerville
and printed in Great Britain by Cox & Wyman Ltd.,
London, Reading and Fakenham
for the publishers, Business Books Limited
(registered office: 180 Fleet Street London EC4)
publishing office: Mercury House, Waterloo Road, London SE1 8UL

Made and printed in Great Britain

To my Mother

CONTENTS

CHAPTER ONE

WHY HELP HIM?

So you're married to a businessman? And what are you doing about it? Are you shutting yourself up at home, pulling up the drawbridge and sealing yourself off completely from your husband's business life? Do you expect him to deposit his business worries on the other shore before he crosses the moat into his castle? Or do you leave the drawbridge always down to act as a causeway between the home and the business world beyond?

Do you help your husband in his career, encourage him to bring his problems home and unburden them to you when he feels a need to? Do you actively help him by being a gracious hostess to his business contacts? Do you, in fact, feel that a man's home life should be completely cut off from his work or do you prefer to be a part of *all* his life?

Perhaps you had not realised how much a woman can really help a man in his career—help or hinder, that is. A well-worn saying tells us that behind every successful man there's a devoted woman. Nothing could be more true and examples of this state of affairs are legion. You no doubt know of several, at various levels, from Sir Winston Churchill and his devoted Clemmie to the little woman down the road you always see sending her husband off to work with a cheerful smile.

The converse is equally true and we have all seen men who have failed to reach their full potential because of unresponsive wives who had no confidence in their men and did not give them the support they needed.

Mark you, we're not suggesting for one moment that you *should* act as aide-de-camp to your businessmen husband. You might feel: 'His business is *his* job. Let him get on with it. I'll take care of the home.' But perhaps, on the other hand, the matter might bear further investigation, so let's see, what's in it for you? Why should you lend a helping hand?

To deal first with the crassly materialistic side of things, the reason here is obvious: if you help to further your husband's career you will be the first to benefit when he moves on to a more highly paid job. *You* will share the larger house, the more expensive car, the fancy holidays abroad, the boat, maybe. And, of course, hand in hand with these things, there will be better clothes for you, more money to spend and that greater ease and relaxation which money brings with it.

Second only to material gains is, of course, the prestige that goes with being the managing director's wife, or the chairman's wife or indeed a director's wife.

Yet the advantages of being a 'supportive' wife, as one sociologist dubs the wife who helps her husband in his career, are by no means confined to the material. On the contrary. If you take an interest in your husband's business, both in general and in detail, you will discover that it is singularly interesting. Why would he be in it otherwise? And what interests him can also interest you. There is absolutely nothing complicated about business. It is chiefly a question of making things and selling things and, above all, whatever line he happens to be in, dealing with people—and people, of course, are infinitely interesting.

So once you begin to find out what your husband is up to during business hours; once you start lending an ear to his problems; once you start meeting the people he has to deal with, your life will become infinitely more interesting and you will learn a great deal about human nature into the bargain. You will find yourself having hunches your husband never even dreamed of and seeing through people where he has been taken in. You will find yourself seeing a problem which seems to baffle the dear man as crystal clear because you have looked straight through it with your clear woman's insight. And of course he will be irritated when this happens.

Indeed if your husband is a really good businessman—and there are not many of them about—then you will learn a great deal about business just by listening to him and observing how he works. There are people who have learned almost all there is to know about business simply by observing others at the game.

Really getting in on the game puts you on a completely different plane from the little fool who announces that her husband is 'something in the City' or who says: 'I'm not sure *what* he does but it's something to do with print.'

Moving next to an altogether more altruistic plane, there is no doubt that sharing your husband's workaday life keeps you closer together. Many men live like identical twins and the wife knows only one twin—the home bod. The businessman twin is completely unknown to his wife. He leaves the house in the morning, spends a stimulating, harassing, demanding, gruelling or just plain busy day at the office, then leaves all that behind him to become the placid television-watcher his wife knows in the evening. She knows nothing of his struggles, triumphs and defeats, nothing of his worries, his problems, his conflicts. She may hardly know what he actually does or what it involves.

Such a wife has no point of contact at all with her businessman husband and really only knows half the man and is close only to this half. Is this good enough? Would it not be more desirable to hear all about what happened at the office? About his struggle to put across his advertising programme for the forthcoming season and how he finally won, over the more conservative factions in the company? Or how he struggled valiantly to secure that large order, but fears that Bloggs Limited may have beat him to the draw with a more competitive offer? Or how he intends to outline his reorganisation plan for his department to the chairman? Would such a state of affairs not draw you more closely together and make you feel more part of his life? Only then would you know the whole man and be close to the whole man.

Finally, if you know and are close to the whole man, the business twin and the home twin, the chances of his going off with someone else are diminished. The reasons for this are obvious. A man grows by his work. The constant stimulation of meeting new challenges, solving new problems, meeting and dealing with people are the stuff that growth is made of. If a wife shares these experiences with her man, albeit at a different level and with less intensity, she can grow with him. If she divorces herself from his business life, on the other hand, and has no career of her own, she will tend to stagnate and before she notices it she and that wonderful man she married have grown worlds apart. When she suddenly wakes up to this fact that gulf between her and her man may be too wide to bridge and they will have become total strangers.

So which kind of a wife do you prefer to be? The decision is of course yours. If you want to be the helpful, co-operative understanding, and well-informed businessman's wife, then here's how to do it.

CHAPTER TWO

HOW TO HELP

The role of the businessman's wife is by no means a simple one, as you will soon discover if you decide to take it on. It is a multi-faceted part requiring all the skill and understanding you can muster. It is important that you consider it a role, for it will keep things in perspective for you and help you to realise that there really is nothing at all terrible about entertaining someone you are not particularly fond of.

We all play various roles during the course of our life, although few of us are really aware of it. Yet aware or unaware we step out of one role into another as surely as the actor who knows full well he is *not* the King of Ruritania. A man will, for instance, spend a short while in the morning playing husband and perhaps father, if he has time. Then he will spend the greater part of the day playing sales manager or stockbroker, or buyer. On his way home in the evening he may well stop off at the pub and for a few moments he will play the role of the hearty jovial man-about-town. And there are other roles the average man will play: the daring dashing sportsman, the devil-may-care punter, the thought-ful far-seeing provider. In each of these situations the man will appear quite different. So much so that people who are used to seeing a person in one role only are frequently quite taken aback to meet them in one of their other roles.

It is useful to be aware of this fact, for it enables you to observe yourself and make sure you are playing the role well.

The art of listening

So what does this role of businessman's wife involve? Many things, as we have said. Perhaps one of the most important is to practise the art of listening. One businessman's wife recently interviewed by a sociologist said she felt inadequate because her husband spent a considerable amount of time pouring out his business problems to her and she was incapable of giving him any advice.

Oh, foolish woman! Like so many women she was completely underestimating her worth and wishing she could do something which is quite unnecessary and uncalled for. A woman who can listen intelligently is worth her weight in gold and she should extend her intelligence to appreciating this and not hanker after unnecessary extras.

So let us divide this business of listening into two distinct categories. Let us call the first type of listening 'acting as a sounding board'. Now businessmen, especially top executives, are lonely people. It is lonely up there at the top. They make magnificent plans for the next season, or next year, they think up 'big deals', mentally reorganise the company, acquire subsidiaries, branch out overseas, introduce new products, close down lines which are not selling—all manner of things. Many of these embryonic plans, if not all of them, are strictly secret at first. A man dare not divulge them to a living soul. For one thing his idea may not be quite complete as yet, or he may not yet be sure of his ground. He may simply be *considering* a new plan, may not have decided yet just how to place it before the Board or how to put it to the senior partner or any number of things. Yet he *wants* to mull over the idea. He *needs* to, otherwise it will never come to fruition.

So what does he do if he has the right kind of wife? He brings the idea home and over coffee he begins telling his wife about it. 'I've been wondering whether we ought not to take away our agency from Faisocchi and open up our own branch in Italy', he might begin. 'Really?' you say. Then you continue to listen, attentively and quietly. 'Yes, but the problem is . . .' and hubby will be off pointing out all the snags, the risk that the branch might lose money at first, the cost involved, the fact that Faisocchi may go off and set up a competitive business of his own, or take on hubby's own competitor's line. On and on he will go, hardly pausing for breath. And you will sit quietly and listen. You might pour him some more coffee, but without interrupting his train of thought.

You will not dash up and disappear into the kitchen, for although in your modesty you might imagine you are doing nothing, in point of fact you are fulfilling a very important role. So stay put, listen attentively so that when his eyes rest on yours he knows you are following his argument.

Absolutely all you need do apart from really listening—and this is of course the important point—is make appropriate 'noises' when he pauses for breath. If he asks a rhetorical question, such as: 'But the point is—will Faisocchi take it lying down?' All you need do is murmur: 'M-m, difficult to tell'.

In nine cases out of ten your much burdened husband will conclude by saying something like: 'So the problem I have to solve is: (a) is it worth the risk or (b) would we be better off with the status quo and egging Faisocchi on to greater efforts?' You can now say something quite simple such as: 'Yes, I see your problem. Oh, well, have a cup of coffee on it.' Pour him another cup and he will now be ready to change the subject.

So what have you accomplished? A great deal. By putting the problem into words he has clarified it in his mind and has in fact broken it down into its component parts. His mind is cleared and he is now ready to go on to the next stage, perhaps investigating more closely as to the performance of his Italian agent and the cost of installing his own branch or putting the idea to someone else in the company.

And you, by acting as an intelligent listener, have helped

your husband to reach his conclusions and clear his mind. A top executive cannot function unless he has someone of the utmost confidence on whom he can try his ideas before they jell. The right kind of secretary can carry out this function and so can the right kind of wife. The only other ingredient this function requires is that you exude a feeling of optimism and confidence. Never make negative comments or register pessimism or fear. Your 'noises' should always be encouraging, optimistic and enthusiastic. He will have enough cold water thrown on his ideas in other quarters. You, as his alter ego, must always be confident (in him) and optimistic (for his plans).

Our second type of listening we could call 'acting as a wailing wall'. This type of listening is by no means confined to wives. Friends oblige one another in this way and so do relatives. A skilled form of this type of listening is done by personnel officers and other professional people whose job it is to help people to unburden themselves.

From the listener's point of view it does not really differ from the sounding-board type of listening. The difference lies in the need it fills for the person unburdening himself. Your man may have been irked to death by one of his superiors and yet been obliged to take it and bear up. The tension grows practically unbearable and when he gets home he simply has to get it off his chest. So he begins to tell you all about it. His voice raises and he grows agitated as all the irritation of the day comes back to him. So you listen attentively and say very little, for it is not likely that he will hesitate to go on and tell you all.

Finally the flood-gates will close and calm will return. Perhaps you will feel once again that you have contributed nothing, served no useful purpose, but you must not feel this way, for on the contrary your attentive and patient listening is invaluable and the businessman in particular has very few people to whom he can turn in this way. Employees lower down the ladder unburden themselves to each other, but an executive cannot easily do this and if he bottles up his frustrations the net result will be ulcers or some other psycho-somatic illness.

Of course, your listening will not be confined to your husband alone, but will serve you in good stead at all company functions and when you act as hostess to your husband's customers, business contacts or superiors, as we shall see later.

Keeping informed

In order to make all this listening meaningful to you and to make sure you also find your husband's problems interesting you would do well to learn as much as you can about the company he works for, the type of business it is in and the actual work your husband does. In other words, if he is a sales executive, then you would find it very interesting to learn something about marketing and salesmanship. It may sound dull at the first blush, but in point of fact these subjects are very interesting and far from being beyond the understanding of anyone. There are many books on the subject and no doubt you can borrow some from your husband or you could get one stealthily from the public library. You might even persuade your man to give you a sight of his company's sales manual and, of course, some of the company's sales brochures.

When he pours out his plans and his problems to you, your background knowledge will not only help you to listen more intelligently, but you will find yourself enthralled by the problem itself, rather than bored to tears and itching to 'turn him off'.

Apart from learning about your husband's company and his business, you would find it worth keeping abreast of general developments in the business world and news in general. Obviously, you will have neither the time nor the inclination to delve deeply into these matters. All you need do is to keep 'switched on' when the news bulletin moves on to deal with the latest mergers, board-room struggles and strikes and scan through the business pages of your daily newspaper.

Shining in company

Thus armed you will be in a much better position to shine at
the company functions you attend with your husband and to
be an interesting conversationalist in general. For unquestionably it will be when you meet your husband's associates
and business contacts that it will become apparent whether
you are an asset to his career or a liability.

We shall deal with such occasions in detail in later chap-
ters, but basically, they will be of two types: either you go to
them or they come to you. You will go to them when you
attend company functions such as the annual dinner-dance,
ladies' nights at your husband's technical society or other
organisation, open house at the 'works', whenever you call to
see your husband informally at the office and when you visit
his colleagues and superiors in their home. On such occasions you will be playing the part of guest.

When they come to you, you will obviously be doing your
level best to be the perfect hostess. The frequency of such
occasions will vary a great deal according to the nature of
your husband's work and the company style, but just about
every businessman's wife is sometimes called upon to entertain her man's boss or a special client or other VIP at some
time and you will naturally want to be prepared for such
occasions, however rare they may be.

You may even, on occasion, find yourself entertaining or
otherwise accompanying business associates of your husband's, or more frequently their wives, outside the home. On
such occasions too you will want to do him proud, and, of
course, there is no reason why you should not.

Let us now see what are the prerequisites to your role as
businessman's wife before going on to further details on the
various occasions.

CHAPTER THREE

THE WELL GROOMED WIFE

One of the first very basic prerequisites is that you be well turned out. Obviously this is something you know quite a lot about. As a single girl you were certainly attractive and well dressed and did not fail to catch the eye of the men you came into contact with. The proof of the pudding is that here you are now, married to a businessman.

Now what? Some married women—not all of them, mark you, but some of them—neglect themselves completely, start putting on weight, lose all interest in clothes, let their husband surprise them with curlers in their hair and an old apron on when he gets back from the office until within months of marriage he is beginning to wonder just what happened to the lovely girl he took to the altar.

Other girls react differently. They go on dressing and acting after marriage like the model, typist, student, debutante or whatever they were before marriage. Have *you* ever seriously stopped to consider what you ought to look like now you are a businessman's wife? Has it occurred to you that just as you looked the part of the carefree single girl before, you should now look the part of the businessman's wife? In other words, that when your husband takes you along to his company's annual dinner-dance, he will expect you to look like his wife, not a little model he picked up for the evening.

Obviously, after marriage needs change, your wardrobe requirements will be different, you may need less street clothes, more at-home clothes and, indeed, your own interest in clothes may well change drastically and there's no reason why they should not. You may quite rightly feel that there's no further need to 'dress to kill' and you will be far freer now to please yourself what you wear, so long as you dress the part for your husband on certain occasions.

So this might be an excellent time to review the whole situation so that you can decide what kind of a 'new you' you want to be, bearing in mind that you are now Mrs Businessman and not the Miss you were before.

Health, beauty and stamina

We usually think of health, beauty, and stamina as three separate things, with no connection between them. If we are healthy, we take it for granted. Beauty we think of as something other women have, or something acquired from a paint box and stamina we consider as a gift of the gods to a chosen few.

Nothing could be further from the truth and this wrong thinking is due to a large extent to false values. We have all seen girls in their teens ruining the natural beauty of their hair with bleaches and dyes. Perhaps you yourself were such a girl. And we all know the girl who barely allows herself four or five hours' sleep at night because she cannot bear to leave a party before the very end. Yet what would the bleached and dyed teenager say if we were to point out to her that there is far more beauty in a clean and healthy head of hair in its natural colour than in any bleached or coloured mop? How would the party-goer react if we reminded her that loss of sleep was making her look like a wreck and that eight hours' sleep every night would improve her appearance beyond recognition? You know the answer—we would be dubbed boring fuddy-duddies and worse.

Yet there can be no doubt that health, beauty and stamina

go hand in hand, the one deriving from the other. Beauty shines out from within, it is not superimposed.

The triple aim of health, beauty and stamina can, to a large extent, be pursued in tandem. You can kill not two, but three birds with one stone. And most of the 'recipe' is quite pleasant to follow. The first requirement is to make sure you are getting enough sleep. The old-fashioned idea about getting your beauty sleep is perfectly sound, as your family doctor will confirm. We do not all need the same amount of sleep, of course, but it is wrong to imagine that five or six hours' sleep a night is enough. Eight hours is nearer the mark for most people and if you are honest with yourself you will have no difficulty finding out what your optimum 'ration' of sleep is.

Perhaps as a single girl you found it hard to go to bed at a reasonable hour because there was always another party or a dance to go to and sleep may have seemed a waste of time. Now you are married you may be tempted to finish off this or that chore before turning in. You must resist the temptation and make sure you get a healthful and beautifying night's sleep every night.

The next ingredient in the health and beauty recipe is, of course, diet and, as you well know, this means having enough of the right kinds of food *every day*. As a single girl you had lots of excuses for not feeding yourself properly: you simply didn't have time to eat because you had to dress for the party and you were being picked up at seven. Or there was a lot to do at the office and you felt you had to make do with a sandwich. Or you may have preferred to go shopping in the lunch hour. Why worry with lunch, it's such a bore!

If you want to go on neglecting yourself you can find a host of brand new excuses now. You're alone for lunch, so why bother, it's such a bore to cook for yourself alone. Or—you're having a good dinner with your husband, so why bother with lunch? This is really not good enough and you must make up your mind to treat yourself more kindly.

Lunch alone is not a bore. It can be a time for experiment, for 'dress-rehearsals' with new dishes. It can be a time for enjoying those foods which you love but your man can't stand. You might even arrange to eat with a neighbour; you can cook for her one lunch-time and she can return the compliment the following day. This way you make sure both of you are having a good meal and you get a little companionship at the same time.

Being determined to feed yourself is only half the battle, however. You must also be sure to eat well-balanced meals. Before you got married or soon after you got back from your honeymoon you must have gone into this matter of the well-balanced diet and it is certainly no secret to you that what you need every day is meat, poultry or fish, eggs, milk or cheese, a salad or a serving of green vegetables, fresh fruit and wholemeal bread. You probably make sure you provide your husband with a well-balanced meal, but if you are like many wives you tend to neglect yourself when you're on your own.

Well, for the sake of your health, beauty and stamina, snap out of it and take care of yourself. If you want to learn more about diet and beauty get Evelyn Forbes's book called *Recipe for Beauty*. It throws a refreshingly different light on the subject of feminine beauty.

Of course, it may well be that your problem involves eating too much, rather than too little. Certainly, if you are overweight you will need to cut down on the intake of food. Don't do it haphazardly, though, but see your doctor and follow a diet under his direction. Nothing is less attractive or more ageing than fat and if you are threatened with it, then you will have to be ruthless with yourself, but under medical supervision remember.

Grooming

As you well know, proper grooming begins with the daily bath or shower. Perhaps now that you are married you will be fortunate enough to be able to linger a little longer over your bath after you have seen your man off to his office. Or it may be, on the other hand, that you have children to take care of and your morning seems more of a rush than ever it was. No matter—bathe you must regardless of circumstances and after the bath, of course, a deodorant.

If you are so rushed that you tend to keep on putting off your own toilet until later and later in the morning, then remember that the busier you are the more important it is to attend to your own toilet first of all. It only takes twenty minutes to take a shower and a couple of seconds to apply a deodorant. If you keep on postponing it you will go all through the day looking like a slattern and nothing can be worse for a woman's morale.

YOUR HAIR The hair has been variously described as woman's crowning glory, the poetry of the face, the secret of woman's fascination, one third of a woman's beauty. Even if all this were only partly true—and who can say with certainty?—it certainly makes a good case for taking great care of your hair.

As with beauty in general, so it is with hair. Beautiful hair is healthy hair. Keep it that way by eating well-balanced meals and by regular shampooing. Make sure you are using the right shampoo for your type of hair and do remember that what may have been the right shampoo for you when you were sixteen may no longer be right now. For instance, you may have had greasy hair, but now you may be using a hair colourant or having a permanent wave. Both these treatments make hair drier and in need of a different shampoo. Don't forget to rinse the hair well. It can take quite a long time, especially if you live in a hard-water area. But don't get impatient and persevere until your hair squeaks between your fingers as you squeeze it. Only then can you be sure you have really got rid of the soap. A little vinegar or half a lemon squeezed into the last rinsing water, or indeed one of the rinses on the market, will speed up the process. A well-rinsed head of hair will shine beautifully rather than presenting a dull powdery appearance, as so often happens.

Do not use a fine-toothed comb or a metal one. A tortoiseshell or bone comb is, of course, the best, but not so readily obtainable nowadays. Hair brushes should be of pure bristle, not nylon. Brush your hair every night. Bend forward and brush from the nape of the neck along the whole surface of the hair. Then toss your head back and brush from the front of your head towards the back. You can do this either sitting down or standing. After brushing, give your scalp a good massage. Resting a thumb on each of your temples, place each finger on the scalp and make a circular motion with the tip of each finger, moving the scalp around and around. Gradually move your hands around the front of your head, then back towards the crown, continuing the rotating motion with each finger. After this, begin at the centre back of your head and massage your way to the crown of your head. You will be amazed at the vitality this simple treatment will give to your hair.

The final basic requirement for a beautiful head of hair is an expert cut. It is worth seeking out someone who really knows how to cut and, if necessary, paying a little more for this vital operation. What else you do or have done to your hair after this is entirely optional and will depend on your own preferences and the state of your hair. Certainly if you are wise you will leave bleaches, colourants and even other artifices until your hair really needs them, then, of course, use all the aids available.

HANDS AND NAILS   Nothing could be harder on the hands and nails than housework and especially constant immersion in water and, if you have the patience, you will be well rewarded if you take some simple precautions. The most obvious precaution to take is, of course, to put on gloves for washing up and certain other kinds of housework. Not everyone can be bothered to do this, however, and you may well find yourself with a pair of gloves handy, but never putting them on when you tackle those dishes.

Perhaps a better idea is to train your man to the American idea of doing the dishes himself. After all, why not? It is a small enough contribution to the household chores. So do try this first of all and on those occasions when you must needs do the washing up yourself, why not use a mop? It certainly keeps your hands out of the water more, which is what you need to aim for.

Avoid putting harsh additives into the washing-up water and after washing up or doing the laundry, dry your hands really well and keep a little hand lotion nearby to rub into them every time. For the married woman it is not always practical to don gloves before going to bed, but do seize the opportunity of doing so whenever you can. In spite of all the expensive preparations on the market, glycerine with a few drops of lemon juice or rose water added, is still the best preparation to soften and whiten the hands. If you use this treatment every night and don a pair of cotton gloves you will soon see the difference. If you have to limit the treatment to certain evenings only you could try it during the day at a time when you know you will be able to keep your gloves on for a couple of hours or so.

Manicure your nails once a week. Soap and scrub them either in the washbasin or in a manicure bowl. Dry thoroughly. Apply a cuticle oil or cream and, when the cuticles are soft, press them back with an orange stick. Re-shape the nails, using an emery board rather than a metal nail file. Aim for a perfect oval and leave at least one tenth of an inch of nail extending from the edge of the finger on both sides. Hold the emery board at a slight angle and file in one direction only, from the outside of the nail towards the centre.

After your manicure would be an excellent time to apply your glycerine and rose water, don your gloves and settle down for a couple of hours of peace and quiet. Rub the glycerine in well, massaging each finger as if you were trying to put on a very tight pair of gloves.

Finally, remember that diet counts with nails too. If you want to have fine strong nails, go for a protein-rich diet with plenty of iron, calcium, potassium, Vitamin B and iodine.

FEET   You certainly do not need to be reminded how hard on the feet the housewife's life is. If your feet ache nothing seems right, so pamper them a little. Give them a sprinkle of talcum powder after your daily bath, change socks or stockings every day and give yourself a pedicure once a week. The 'drill' is the same as for hands, the only real difference being that toenails should be cut straight across to prevent them from growing into the flesh.

If you should get a corn, bunion, inward-growing toenail or other trouble, see a chiropodist right away. It is foolish to attempt to be your own foot doctor. Your feet are far too precious to neglect and they are worth all the trouble you may take over them.

One great favour you can do to your feet now that you are married is to wear sensible shoes. You should take the view that it is your *right* to walk freely and comfortably and any attempt to imprison and torture your feet with unnaturally shaped shoes or ridiculously high heels are an impingement on your liberty and an attempt to enslave you. Think about this carefully and you will realise what such fashions are really doing to women.

MAKE-UP   We now come to the icing on the cake. Nothing could be more subject to fashion and custom than make-up. Within the past sixty years we seem to have come full-circle from 'nice' women not wishing to be seen dead *in* lipstick, to not daring to appear in public *without* it and now back again towards not wearing any. Fortunately the times are now ripe for a woman to be able to make up her own mind as to what, if anything, she wants to put on her face. It is most important that you should assert this right and not allow yourself to be bulldozed into either wearing or not wearing make-up.

The important thing to bear in mind is that make-up is not intended to be a mask, although it unfortunately all too frequently is. It is meant to enhance your good points, minimise your blemishes, make the most of what Mother Nature gave you and underscore your individuality. It should be used with discretion and applied with skill. In fact make-up is an art. It requires good taste, skill and knowledge to make-up well.

No doubt you have had a good deal of experience in making up your face and you do it well, but you too must have seen on other women's faces the results of bad taste, lack of skill and sheer ignorance of what is needed. You will also have seen many women, and especially young girls, wearing the wrong kind of make-up for the occasion, such as a garish theatrical 'job' behind an office desk. So you know what to avoid.

Perhaps at one time you took advice, either from one of the beauty salons or quite simply from the beauty counsellor in one of the big stores, on the correct foundation for your type of skin and on the right lipstick and eye-make-up for you. You may be going merrily on using such products and going through the same make-up routine as you did ten years ago. This is a dangerous thing to do, for nothing changes more quickly than fashions in make-up and nothing looks more dated than a lipstick colour which is passé. Moreover our colouring changes over the years and what might have been perfect at sixteen will not look quite so good at twenty and even less suitable at twenty-five. And, of course, if you change your hair colour, your whole make-up will have to change.

DRESS   It may sound dull, but there is no doubt that being well dressed is largely a question of suitability. You should dress to suit the occasion, to suit your type and to suit your figure. If you stop to think about this it will become obvious that, now you are Mrs Businessman you may well need to dress quite differently from when you were a single girl, for now the occasions will be different, your figure may well be different, at least to some extent and your type may have changed too. In other words, you may have decided that you are no longer the gamine type and indeed *every* woman gets beyond the gamine stage, unless she dies prematurely, that is!

Dressing to suit the occasion is not a difficult one to deal with. Your life has changed and your clothes will reflect this change. The chances are you will need fewer but better 'evening out' clothes, far fewer of the type of clothes you used to wear at your daily occupation and more hostess gowns and other 'at-home' clothes. And you will now be freed from the nightmare of leaving the house in the morning, dressed for the office or what have you, but carrying 'spare parts' to make a quick transformation for an evening date.

As for dressing according to your type, it will involve making up your mind whether you are still the same type as you were before. You may be, of course, in which case no great transformation scenes will be needed. If you were the well-tailored girl, then there is no reason why you should not remain so. If you were the athletic outdoor girl, then you will no doubt continue to be so. If, on the other hand, you were the gamine type, or the little girl type, then obviously it is time to grow up and you will have to take a good objective look at yourself and decide what you want to be in the next act.

As for dressing according to your figure, this is frequently determined by your type, so you can kill two birds with one stone. The athletic outdoor girl is not infrequently statuesque and the fragile, very feminine girl is frequently quite petite. But it is not always so easy and where type and figure do not go hand in hand, you will also need to bear your figure in mind.

If you are petite, keep everything in scale, that is, small. A small woman with an enormous handbag looks ridiculous. A huge hat likewise looks ridiculous on her. Large prints, very high heels and skirts flopping around your calves are also not for you, if you are petite. Above all, if you are petite, don't rebel against it. Give in and *be* petite.

If you are very tall, don't fight it by drooping. You cannot disguise your height by slouching, so stand tall. You can wear fairly large patterns and, if you are tall and slim, horizontal stripes. Wear medium high heels and hats and bags which are neither tiny nor enormous. Floor-length dresses look tremendous on you.

If you are stocky, avoid voluminous skirts, especially if they are gathered at the waist, wide collars and sleeves and anything else which gives you added width. Avoid cutting yourself in half with contrasting jackets or bodices and go instead for the slender line, the small hat and medium heels.

If you are large busted you can wear deep round or square necklines or a 'V' neckline, but under no circumstances should you be tempted by the Empire line. Anyone without a tiny bust looks absolutely awful in it.

It is difficult to give an impression of elegance if you combine too many colours. Use no more than two at a time, plus one or more neutrals, which are black, white, brown, and beige. Remember, however, that your hair counts as a colour, so if you are a redhead you cannot afford to wear more than one other colour, plus one or more neutrals.

Your choice of a colour scheme will obviously depend upon your colouring and only seeing the colours against you in daylight will really tell you if they suit you. But here is a general guide, though it is as well to bear in mind that there is more than one school of thought on this matter of what goes with what.

If you are a fair-skinned blonde with blue or grey eyes the pastels are for you: powder blue, aquamarine, lilac, rose pink, yellow. All shades of beige look equally stunning on blondes, used as a monotone colour scheme or in combination with another colour.

If you are a dark-eyed blonde who tans easily, wear darker shades of the colours mentioned, that is, cornflower blue, geranium red, sunshine yellow.

If your hair is brown flamboyant shades are for you. Try coral, apricot, orange, gold and choose navy blue or brown as your basic colour.

If you are a true brunette with black or nearly black hair try emerald green, shocking pink, royal blue. If your eyes are green or blue, key your costume to your eyes. Nothing could be more striking.

If you are a redhead always let your hair be the predominant colour and use only one other colour. Try browns, russet, gold, grey-green, some shades of yellow.

ACCESSORIES   As we have seen, your accessories should be in keeping with the rest of your outfit, a tailored bag with a suit, a straw or fabric pouch with a print dress, *never* a straw hat with a fur coat, of course; preferably a shoulder bag with a trouser suit. Match accessories for colour or type of material in two's, for instance match hat to gloves, bag to gloves, or shoes to gloves. Bags and shoes can frequently be bought as a set, but in any event, if you have black patent leather shoes, then have a handbag of the same material, never suede, for instance. If the shoes are suede, then have a suede handbag too.

Fortunately things have relaxed a great deal also in the matter of accessories and it is perfectly in order nowadays to be seen abroad minus hat and minus gloves on most occasions. Indeed, if you always go around dressed to the nines, in hat, gloves, and handbag you risk looking a touch old-fashioned. So providing you always wear shoes you need not really suffer any loss of sleep as to what to wear on this or that occasion. Use your own discretion and chances are that all will be well.

Clothes care

The finest clothes in the world will not look well on you for long, neither will they last if you do not give them the care and attention they need. Regular dry cleaning is a must and there is no excuse nowadays for not making regular pilgrimages to the dry cleaner's. If you have spilled something on a garment, try to remember what it was and let the cleaner know, as this will help him to decide how to treat the stain. If you perspire heavily, ask the cleaner to give special attention to the area under the arms.

Keep a spot remover handy for emergencies. If you splash a drop of fat on your dress, sprinkle talcum powder on it right away. Later on, brush off the powder and you will find that the stain has gone with it.

Always brush and hang suits and dresses as soon as you take them off. Press skirts regularly, using a damp cloth for woollens. Fill a saucer with water, add a few drops of clear ammonia, dip your clothes brush in the liquid and brush skirts and jackets before ironing.

Always replace buttons and stitch hanging hems before hanging any garment up. Make a point of sewing tapes and press-studs in all new blouses and dresses as soon as you bring them home from the shop. If you are especially lazy you can buy tapes with a safety-pin already attached, but certainly a popper is neater.

Clean both shoes and handbags regularly and take these opportunities of making sure your shoes are not down at heel.

At the end of a season, clean all your shoes and have necessary repairs made, wash and iron all washables and send the remaining garments to the dry-cleaners. Store everything away, covering all garments with plastic or other covers. You will find it a great relief, when that season comes around again to find everything in order and ready to wear, with little more than a light iron.

CHAPTER FOUR

HOW ARE YOUR MANNERS?

Nothing gives a person greater confidence than knowing what to do in any situation. Such a person exudes ease and *savoir faire* and is the envy of her friends. If you wanted to set yourself a triple aim, you could do no better than to:

try to feel at ease with everyone, whether cabbage or king and conversely to make both cabbages and kings feel at ease with you;

try to be thoughtful and gracious with everyone, no matter how lowly—the truly well-mannered person is recognised by the way she treats humble people to whom she is beholden for nothing;

try to let nothing embarrass you. The wise woman is never embarrassed.

If you do all of these things you will be a person with good manners. The essence of good manners is thoughtfulness and consideration for others; they have currency all over the world.

What then of etiquette? Etiquette is a set of agreed conventions governing our relations with others. They differ somewhat from country to country and what may be the 'done thing' in Britain could well turn out to be taboo somewhere on the Continent or in the U.S.A. Since there can be no etiquette without good manners, it might be best to think of etiquette as a subsidiary of good manners. In case of conflict, then good manners always takes precedence over etiquette.

There is a story about King Edward VII which illustrates this point most eloquently. The King was entertaining a distinguished guest from India. Asparagus was served and the King noticed that his guest was eating the edible tips of the vegetable and tossing the hard stalks over his shoulder. The King promptly followed suit as if he had been eating asparagus that way all his life and in this way saved his guest from possible embarrassment. A thoughtful gesture indeed!

Today we are faced with two situations which threaten to upset our whole concept of how to behave. First of all we have the great revolt of the young against convention and just about everything else. In the case of good manners and etiquette they have tended to throw out the baby with the bath water, their judgement being too poor to differentiate between basic essentials and outmoded frills. The second situation is the fact that everyone is travelling more. We ourselves go abroad either on business or pleasure bent, our children take school trips abroad. Some of us spend several months working on the Continent and many Continentals come over here. After many years of receiving American tourists, we have finally started to return the compliment and it is not unusual to hear of people popping over to the States for two or three weeks.

This twin situation means that, on the one hand we see a great disregard for the rules of etiquette from many of our own young people, and on the other hand we are coming into contact with people from other parts of the world who follow different rules, at least in some respects.

What line are you to take then? It is quite simple, really, for there is only one way out. Continue to be thoughtful and courteous to all, while relaxing somewhat on points which are purely convention and cannot harm anyone. Let your touchstone be this: would your proposed action cause dis-

comfort, embarrassment or annoyance to those present? If
the answer is 'yes' or even 'maybe', then don't do it. If your
proposed action can harm no one, then go ahead and do it
and let the pieces fall where they may.

Above all, do not be snobbish about etiquette or feel superior because you happen to know how to use the snail
tongs or, worse yet, embarrassed because you *don't* know
how to use them. There is another asparagus story which
illustrates admirably how unimportant such things really are
and how foolish it is to be embarrassed by them.

The story takes place in a British Rail dining car. A man
comes in and sits down. A woman, obviously from the
country, follows and sits down opposite him. In due course
the steward serves both of them with asparagus. The country
woman eyes hers with some misgivings, then turns to her
fellow-traveller and asks: 'How on earth does one eat
these?'

Oh, admirable woman!

Introductions

In any event, the important things to remember in the
streamlined mores of today, are not many and you can soon
put right any flaws in your behaviour. One small ceremony
which it is useful to become adept at is introductions. As a
businessman's wife you no doubt meet a great many of your
husband's business associates and prospective clients and you
certainly want to be at ease when being introduced to
them.

The rules are simplicity itself. Men are introduced to
women, juniors to seniors, both men and women to eminent
personages. The two exceptions are that members of one's
own family are introduced to those outside the family and
everyone, whether man or woman, is presented to Royalty.

In theory this means that, when introducing two women,
you introduce the younger to the elder or the lower ranking

to the higher ranking, likewise with two men. In practice, however, it is not always easy to tell which is the elder, especially where women are concerned and again, it does not follow that it is a mortal sin to fail to give precedence to the 31-year-old lady over her 'junior' aged 30! So do not worry unduly about this one unless the gap is obvious enough for all to see. Rank is usually easier to tell and you probably won't have many problems of this nature, anyhow.

The old-fashioned way to introduce two people to each other is to say: 'May I present Mr So-and-So?' This is no longer done, except in the case of Royalty. In fact introductions are becoming casual to the point where a great many people simply say: 'John, this is Alan Greene. John Smeaton.' A slight touch of formality does linger on in business circles, however, at any rate in *some* business circles. In such circles they may say: 'Mr Smith, may I introduce Mr Eldridge? Henry Smith.' Or quite simply: 'John, this is Mr Eldridge. John Brown.' It is quite clear from these two last examples who is being introduced to whom. This is quite a good dodge if you are unsure of getting it right. If you first address the person to whom you are making the introduction, then you are sure of getting it right. Otherwise you can simply mention the two names: 'Mr Smith. Mr Brown.' This would be rather bald if you only had two people to introduce, but if there were several, then it would be quite adequate.

It is always a good idea to add a word or two of amplification. It gives the two strangers a thread on which to hang a conversation. You might say, for instance: 'Mr Smith, may I introduce Mr Brown? He's also interested in archaeology, you know.' Or: 'He's just flown in from Geneva.' The worthy Mr Smith can then volley right back with: 'Are you *really*?' Or: 'Did you *really*?' The ice is broken and they're off. Otherwise they might wonder just what to say after they've mumbled 'How d'you do?'

After the introduction has been made the two people concerned say 'How d'you do', usually simultaneously. It is the only correct formula in Britain. On no account should you say 'Pleased to meet you', 'I'm very well, thank you', or 'Hallo'. It's just one of those crazy British customs which it is useless to argue with. It does have the merit of simplicity, for it leaves no room for doubt. That's what you should say and no further doubt need assail you. It is rather a cold formula, so do smile as you say it and try to put a little friendliness into your voice, especially when meeting people from overseas.

As a woman you have no obligation to shake hands as you say 'How d'you do?' A nod and a smile is all that is needed. It is supposed to be a sign of special friendliness to proffer your hand, so if you feel a little warmth and friendliness is in order, then by all means offer your hand. Two men being introduced always shake hands.

A woman does not need to rise to acknowledge an introduction. A man always does. If he is wearing gloves, he takes one off before shaking hands. A woman does not.

REMEMBERING NAMES   We all like the sound of our own name. In fact it is our favourite sound. Yet how inept the British are at remembering other people's names. You will certainly have noticed, on the other hand, how good Americans are at remembering people's names. How do they do it? They have a number of little secrets. One of them is to repeat the name of the person immediately upon introduction. They will say: 'How d'you do, Mr Sinclair?' In this way the name is fixed in their memory. If necessary, they will jot the name down at the first opportunity.

If the name is a difficult one, an American will say: 'Marjoribanks? That's an interesting name. How do you spell it?' Nothing could be more useful for fixing a name in your memory.

An American will never hesitate to remark that your name sounds rather Italian, or Spanish, or Russian or to go into a little conversation about it, but this kind of thing tends to embarrass the British.

Another technique is association of ideas. 'Fish' might make you remember Mr Mish's name, for instance. It seems to work wonders for some people, but has disastrous results for others, so tread cautiously with this one.

Whatever you do afterwards, do not fail to listen when someone is being introduced to you. If you really do, then it is not so difficult to remember. And if you are doing the introducing, then pronounce the names clearly and audibly.

Regardless of how conscientious you are, however, and how well you do your homework, the day will dawn when you find yourself about to introduce someone whose name completely escapes you. You know her as well as the back of your hand. You've probably known her for years, but try as you may you simply cannot recall her name. The closer the dreaded moment gets the more agitated you become, but rack your brain as you will, the name simply will not come. So what to do? There is one gambit you can try and very frequently it works. You can say to the other person: 'Jane, this is . . .' and nine times out of ten your acquaintance will spring right in to your rescue and say her name. If she does not, then you will have to let your voice trail off and add *sotto voce*: 'I do apologise, but I've completely forgotten your name.' Not very flattering to your acquaintance with whom you were chatting so amiably a moment previously, but there it is, perfection is not of this world and she will undoubtedly forgive you.

If it is a man you want to introduce to your acquaintance, then, of course, this gambit won't do and you'll have to say something like: 'I simply must introduce Mr So-and-So to you, but I'm afraid I've forgotten your name.'

If it is only the surname you've forgotten, then you're not on such a sticky wicket. You simply say: 'What *is* your surname, Joan? It's just escaped me for a second.'

All of us experience this difficulty from time to time, so do be alert and bail others out by saying your name if you see signs of the other person having forgotten it. You can usually tell by their eyes. They look like a frightened deer if they have forgotten your name at the strategical moment. They will be most grateful to you if you promptly say your name. Then they can pretend they knew it all along.

GROUP INTRODUCTIONS It quite often happens that you have to introduce one person to a whole group. This will certainly happen when you are entertaining in your home. The form is quite simple: announce the name of the newcomer and then lead him to each person in the group in turn, saying their name as you go: 'Mr Smith, Mrs Smith, Miss Gibbs,' and so on. As the party grows bigger, however, you will only confuse a newcomer by taking her around to meet a large number of people, none of whom she knows. In such cases, lead her up to a small group whom you feel might be congenial and introduce the newcomer to that smaller group only.

At a party do not unnecessarily break up a group which seems absorbed in order to introduce a newcomer. Rather, lead the new arrival to anyone alone or to a small group which is not quite so absorbed. Above all, however, never greet new arrivals and then leave them to their own devices, unless you are quite sure they know several others present.

INTRODUCING YOURSELF If you find yourself sitting next to a strange man at a dinner party, he will usually introduce himself. Return the compliment by saying simply: 'I'm Mary Brown.' If it is a company event, you will in all probability know your table partners, but if not, by all means introduce yourself. You might add, 'Bob Brown's wife.'

At very large parties it is perfectly in order to speak to people without a formal introduction, but never hesitate to say who you are if you find there is an uneasy feeling in the air.

At the table

Another area you will want to check up on is the question of
table manners, for nothing can let you down so badly as
clumsy behaviour at the table.

Generally speaking, table manners are a set of conventions with no rhyme or reason, plus just a small admixture
of good habits which take into account the feelings and
comfort of your fellow diners. The latter are very important
indeed and, like all matters pertaining to good manners, are
applicable throughout the civilised world. These good habits
include eating with your mouth closed where at all possible,
eating silently, keeping your elbows close to your sides so as
not to poke your neighbour's ribs, refraining from smoking
until the end of the meal, and not speaking of subjects un-
suited to meal times, such as operations, diseases and so on.

The purely conventional half of table manners varies from
country to country and no one is expected to switch eating
habits every time he crosses a frontier. The British are
perhaps the neatest eaters in the world, but at the same time
the saddest diners of them all, for one seldom sees an Eng-
lishman looking as if he is enjoying his meal. In fact one can
almost hear an old-fashioned Englishwoman admonishing
her child: 'Well-bred children don't *enjoy* their food.'

It really would be a blessing if we could unbend at table to
the point of looking as if we were enjoying our meals, while
still maintaining our good eating habits.

Some English taboos are positively sadistic. For instance,
it is supposed to be utterly vulgar to crook your little finger
as you lift your tea cup. Yet if you look at this gesture without prejudice you will find it looks quite graceful and in any
event it hurts no one. But before you wax rebellious and
decide that henceforth you shall assert your right to crook
your little finger if you want to, do bear this in mind: if your
husband is a junior executive and you crook your little finger
rebelliously at the next company event, you can be sure that
some crusty old dowager, the chairman's wife in all prob-

ability, will hiss ominously behind her fan: 'Who's that vulgar little woman crooking her finger?' And you will be branded as not quite up to snuff.

So it's 'Down, boy' for little fingers. If it's any consolation to you, fingers neatly tucked by the side of your cup give you better leverage and make the cup easier to support. A far more important point is always to remember to pick up cup and saucer together, hold saucer in your left hand at chest level and take your cup in your right hand. Never, ever leave your saucer on the coffee table and let your cup travel all the way from table to your mouth without the saucer underneath to catch any drops which may fall. This, of course, only applies when having tea or coffee from a low table.

For main meals the approved British eating drill is as follows: shake out your napkin and place it across your lap. This is simplicity itself with a beautiful damask napkin, but if you are having to make do with a paper affair, then it will slip off your lap time and time again and you could find yourself dithering all through the meal in a valiant attempt to keep your napkin on your lap. If you are wearing a low-slung belt or something of this nature, you will have to try surreptitiously tucking a corner of the napkin into it. If, on the other hand, you are wearing a rather short skirt, you can tuck the napkin under the hem, although it won't be a great deal of help, you will find. The only other expedient you can resort to is pinioning down the napkin with your evening bag.

If you are having a meal in a restaurant, you will find the cutlery placed beside your plate in the order in which you are to use it. Assuming a meal of soup, fish, meat and dessert, you will find on your right, moving from the outside inwards: soup spoon, fish knife, meat knife. On your left you will find fish fork and meat fork. In most restaurants dessert spoon and fork and bread knife are placed one below the other at the top of the cover.

In a restaurant, if you have not ordered the fish, for instance, the waiter will remove the fish knife and fork, thus clearing up the confusion a little. At home, you will obviously know what you are going to serve and will set the table accordingly.

The first course may very well be not soup, but some kind of starter and quite often the appropriate eating irons will be brought along with it. Otherwise they will be by the side of the plate, before the soup spoon. This is precisely what gets some people flustered. They use the wrong implement for the first course, then find themselves with nothing but the butter knife with which to tackle the steak. Should this happen to you, be not dismayed: if you are hostess running your own show, simply motion to the waiter and ask for a steak knife. If you are a guest, or otherwise escorted by a man, ask *him* to galvanise the waiter into action. If you are entertaining in your own home, be alert to such gaffes on the part of your guests and see that replacements are provided as needed without their having to ask.

Salt and mustard should be placed on the side of the plate, never sprinkled directly on to the food. Sprinkling salt all over your food used to be considered the height of vulgarity in Britain, while in France it is considered an insult to the hostess, for she is supposed to have used just exactly the right amount of condiment so that no further additions are needed at table. There is a story about an offended French dowager who reproved a salt-sprinkling guest with the words: 'Chez moi on cuisine dans la cuisine!' There is some truth in the French view and a hostess who has spent several hours in the kitchen bringing her dishes to perfection for her guest, does indeed feel slighted if the first thing a guest does when served is to sprinkle her whole plate with salt. So do try to make a habit of leaving the condiments where they are, tasting your food and only if you find any need, reaching for the salt. This applies more particularly when dining in a private home and comes under the heading not of etiquette but of thoughtful behaviour towards your hostess.

Nowadays, of course, many dining tables, both in restaurants and in homes, sport giant pepper and salt mills.

These, obviously, have to be ground over the food, if needed, and there's no remedy for it.

Butter is placed on the side of the bread plate, never directly on the bread. Break your roll with your hands, then break off small pieces and butter them as needed. Do not butter half a roll and bite a bit off, as if it were a slice of bread and butter. Incidentally, breakfast marmalade or jam should likewise be put on the side of the plate and not directly on to the bread and butter.

Salads go on a special salad plate or bowl, if provided, otherwise on the meat plate. Sauces and gravy can go either directly on to the food, or on the side, but mashing your food into the gravy is strictly taboo. Mopping up the gravy with bread, a favourite Continental pastime, is strictly taboo in Britain, but there are those who choose to defy this nonsensical rule. As a businessman's wife, however, never forget that the chairman's lady's beady eye is upon you and beware!

Between mouthfuls, rest knife and fork across your plate, roughly at right-angles to each other. On no account should you rest them on the table cloth. When you have finished a course, place knife and fork neatly together on your plate. If you are dining in a restaurant, this will tell the waiter that you have finished. There are supposed to be two schools of thought as to whether the tines of the fork and the bowl of the spoon should be turned upwards or downwards, but this momentous question surely does not merit undue attention.

When you have finished eating, leave the plate exactly where it is. It may be tempting to push it away, but this is definitely not done.

At a large banquet where several wines are being served, you will find the glasses arranged in exactly the same way as the cutlery, that is, in the order in which they are to be used. Always bring your napkin to your mouth before taking a drink of wine and signal discreetly to the waiter if you do not wish your glass to be refilled.

As for the various edibles, they should be tackled as follows.

APPLES AND PEARS   On formal occasions, these should be speared with the fork, cut into quarters, cored and peeled, then cut into smaller pieces and eaten with fruit knife and fork. At more down-to-earth occasions, this fruit is usually eaten with the fingers after cutting and coring.

ARTICHOKES   They are served either hot with an individual dish of melted butter, or cold with a dish of vinaigrette. Lift off each leaf, dip the edible-tip in the sauce provided and bite it off. Lift off the small white leaves left in the centre and scrape away the choke below them. Eat the heart with a knife and fork.

ASPARAGUS   There just seems to be no end to the asparagus stories. The latest one is culled from *The Daily Telegraph*. The scene is a Foreign Office reception. Says one woman to another: 'But how d'you *know* he's not our sort?' 'By the way he eats his asparagus', replies the other woman, 'he holds it as though he were playing darts'.

Asparagus is actually a very simple vegetable to eat. It is eaten with the fingers. It is usually served with melted butter or a sauce. Simply pick up the asparagus with your fingers, dip the green tip into the butter or sauce provided, bite off the tip, then place the hard inedible part on the side of your plate. If the asparagus is very thin and overcooked, you will have to eat it with a fork and this is, in fact, the more modern practice. Many American restaurants supply tongs to pick up asparagus.

AVOCADO PEAR   It is served halved, with the stone removed and the hollow filled with a sauce, vinaigrette, prawns, crabmeat, or with a wedge of lemon, which you squeeze into the pear. Eat it with a spoon.

CAVIARE   It is served with toast, butter and lemon. Butter the toast, squeeze lemon on the caviare, and pile a mouthful at a time on to the toast, which you then eat with your fingers.

CHEESE   Soft cheese is spread on to biscuit or bread, hard cheese is balanced, a mouthful at a time, on to biscuit or bread. The Continental practice of eating cheese with a knife and fork is gaining popularity.

CORN ON THE COB   There is no elegant way of eating this vegetable. It is sometimes served with a skewer stuck into each end. In such cases, pick it up by the skewers with both hands and bite off the corn from end to end. You will previously have spread the corn with butter and added salt and pepper to taste. If no skewers are provided, just pick up the cob with your fingers and tuck in.

CURRY   It is served with a spoon and fork. Eat it as you would a pudding.

GRAPES AND CHERRIES   Deposit the pips and cherry stones into your closed fist and funnel them on to your plate. If the cherries are cooked, you can sometimes separate the stones while on the plate. Failing this, remove them from your mouth on to your spoon.

GULLS' EGGS   They are served hard-boiled in their shells, four or five to a dish or basket. Pick one up, crack it on the side of your plate, shell it, dip it into salt and eat it with your fingers.

JELLY   Eat it with spoon and fork or spoon alone. Never with fork alone.

LOBSTER   It is usually served in the half-shell, with claws and mayonnaise nearby. Eat the lobster with your fish knife and fork, or fork only, dipping each piece into the sauce. Hold claw in your left hand and dig flesh out with the special lobster pick provided, or with your fish fork.

MELON   Whether a half melon or a slice it is served with sugar, ground ginger, cinnamon, lemon, or draped with paper-thin slices of Parma ham. Sprinkle the melon with the condiments provided and eat it with a spoon if a half or with a knife and fork if a slice. If you are having it with Parma ham, do eat the two together, as they make a delicious combination.

MUSSELS   They are served in a dish in their own broth. The most formal way of eating them is to use fork and spoon, forking the fish on to the spoon and eating it together with a little of the broth. The slightly less formal way is to pick up the shells with your fingers and take out the mussel with your fork, finally drinking the broth with a spoon.

OLIVES   Use fingers if no *hors d'oeuvre* picks are provided. If the olive has a stone, pass it from your mouth into your fist and funnel it from there on to your plate or nearest suitable receptable. Olive stones can become a problem because not infrequently there are no suitable receptables anywhere within striking distance, so plan a strategy before accepting an olive.

ORANGE   Spear it with a fork held in the left hand, quarter it and peel it with your knife, separate the segments, remove the pips and eat the segments one at a time. On less grand occasions it is more usual to use fingers and knife for this tricky operation. In some countries they serve oranges ready peeled and they are then eaten with knife and fork, cutting right through the orange rather than segmenting it.

OYSTERS   They are served by the dozen or the half-dozen, on the half-shell around a plate, sometimes on ice.

They are accompanied by brown bread and butter, lemon and red pepper. Squeeze the lemon on the oysters, sprinkle on some red pepper and eat them with the special fork provided. On less formal occasions it is perfectly in order to drink the liquor from the shell, if you like it.

PÂTÉ DE FOIE GRAS The genuine article is made from specially fattened goose liver, but most *pâté de foie* served nowadays has never been within miles of a goose. Regardless of authenticity, however, it is eaten in the same way. It is served with toast. Spread the *pâté* on the toast, a mouthful at a time.

PRAWNS If served in their shells, shell them with your fingers and dip them in the accompanying sauce, brandishing them by the tail. If they are served already shelled, eat them with a fork.

PEACHES Spear with a fork held in the left hand and peel with a fruit knife. Cut small pieces from around the stone and eat them with the fork.

PEAS Hold your fork in your left hand with the tines pointing downwards, then press the peas against the back of the fork with your knife. You will unhappily find that some peas are too hard for this treatment and will have to guide them on to your fork with your knife instead.

SCALLOPS They are served in their own shells. Eat them with a fork.

SNAILS This French delicacy can be a trap for the unwary. They are served six to a dozen in a special round dish and a pair of tongs and a two-pronged fork are provided. Seize each snail with the tongs in the left hand and extract the snail with the special fork. It is perfectly in order to turn the shell upside down and let out all the garlic butter, which is then mopped up with bread. Do go carefully otherwise your snail will rocket off your plate and perhaps land in your dining partner's lap. Even worse has been known to happen, so beware.

SPAGHETTI   The only correct way to eat spaghetti is with a fork only, held in the right hand. Stick the fork sideways into the spaghetti, twirl a reasonable amount around the fork and eat them. Don't panic if some of the spaghetti refuse to be docile. It happens all the time in Italy. You simply coax them with the greatest nonchalance into your mouth. In spite of the number of people who do it, on both sides of the Channel, it is not correct to twirl your spaghetti around your fork against the bowl of a spoon held in the left hand. This is classified as a *petit bourgeois* habit in Italy and, obviously, you'd rather be dead than branded as such, so do refrain. In any event, this method is definitely no easier than the other. One point to bear in mind when cooking spaghetti in your own home is to have them the right length, which means breaking them once through the middle. This gives you the right length for eating. Incidentally, to serve spaghetti from a bowl take a fork in each hand, lift up a serving of spaghetti and bring them right clear of the bowl before transferring them on to a plate. And do remember that spaghetti are plural.

SOUP   Soup served from a plate or a bowl should be taken from the side of the spoon. Tilt the plate away from you to take the last drop. Clear soup, known as *consommé*, if served in a cup may be drunk out of a cup or with a spoon. Usually one takes a few spoonfuls and when it is cool enough, one drinks the rest from the cup. A *consommé* cup is lifted with both hands, one on each handle, of course.

WATER MELON   The very best way to eat water melon is to brandish a slice with both hands and bury your head into it, but this would never do, of course. The slices are usually served already cut at intervals, so all you need do is spear each mouthful with your fork, held in the left hand, pull away the pips with your knife held in the right hand and then eat.

WHITEBAIT Served with lemon wedge and bread and butter. Squeeze lemon on the tiny fish and eat whole, head and all.

Some people reserve their table manners for special occasions or when someone else is looking. Consequently they never look comfortable when eating in company. This is bad practice on a number of counts. Sitting down at a carefully laid-up table and eating a well prepared meal is all part and parcel of being civilised, it is part of our culture. It is not, or should not be, a display.

So if you do not do so already, try to make a practice, even when having lunch at home, completely on your own, of setting the table carefully and of eating correctly. It takes no longer and is infinitely more enjoyable.

CHAPTER FIVE

PLAYING SOCIAL SECRETARY

As a businessman's wife you will almost certainly take care of the details concerning your social life together, in some instances acting in tandem with your husband's secretary. You will probably find this a most enjoyable occupation, even though it will perhaps involve entertaining people you yourself do not particularly care for.

One of the most important tools in organising your social life is the engagement diary. Have a large one on your desk or wherever you do your paper work and keep it there all the time. If you have more private engagements than you can keep in your head, then you will need a smaller diary for your handbag. Every time you make an entry in the large diary, make a point of transferring it to your pocket diary and, conversely, if you have made an appointment while out of the house, be sure to transfer it to the large diary as soon as you get home. In this way you will avoid finding yourself with two different things to do at the same time.

Occasionally your husband's secretary will phone up about a ladies' night or other social event you are invited to with your husband and then you can enter it in both diaries. She will certainly mention what dress is called for, but should she forget, make sure you ask and then jot that too down in the diaries. Normally, social invitations are accepted on a first-come, first-served basis and one is also free to decline if one wishes to. When it comes to social affairs connected with your husband's business, however, there may be occasions when you will have to cancel a previously made engagement in order to accommodate them and you will also do well not to beg off just because you'd rather not go. This is just one of the penalties of being a business-man's wife.

Visiting cards

Another useful tool is the visiting card. It should be engraved on good quality card, not letterpress printed. This means that you will have to have a plate made. It is rather a costly business, but once you have the plate you can keep on re-using it almost indefinitely.

Whether you have a card for yourself and another one for you and your husband jointly is really entirely up to you. The elaborate ritual of card-leaving and calling is now a thing of the past, although it is still practised in some circles. Consequently cards are not used nearly so much as they used to be.

However, should you want to have two sets of cards, both of them have to be of the same size, that is, $3\frac{5}{8}$ in. × $2\frac{5}{8}$ in. Your own card should read Mrs John Brown, never, of course, Mrs Muriel Brown, and the double card should read Mr and Mrs John Brown. The prefix 'Hon.' is never used on visiting cards, neither are personal qualifications, orders, degrees and decorations. The name goes in the centre of the card, the address in the bottom left-hand corner, and the telephone number in the bottom right-hand corner.

There are a number of type-faces you can use and the stationer from whom you order the cards will show you several. A safe choice is copperplate script. Black borders to indicate a bereavement are no longer used.

Although the practice of leaving cards has all but disappeared, you will still find your card quite useful. You can use it to accompany a bouquet of flowers or other gift, to give your address to a new friend, to scribble a short note, to slip through the door if you have called on a friend and found her out.

The use of visiting cards for these new purposes has been gaining considerable ground during recent years and since some of these purposes require more space, a new type of card has appeared, thought up by the Americans, it would seem. It is called an 'informal' and consists of a sort of double visiting card, folded at the top with the back half blank. This gives you plenty of space on which to write a message. If you have informals engraved, they can be printed from the same plate as the cards. You would do well to have matching envelopes, but do bear in mind that the smallest Post Office preferred envelope size is 5½ in. × 3½ in. and your envelope will therefore have to be somewhat larger than necessary. If this irks you, you could have an envelope to fit the card and a larger one for use through the mails only. An informal card is shown in Fig. 1.

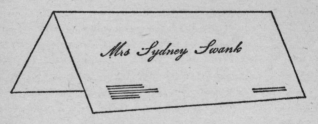

Figure 1 The informal card

Invitation cards

Fortunately, when it comes to invitation cards the old rule about having them engraved no longer holds and only the real sticklers for convention, who happen to be well heeled to boot, bother about it. Wedding invitations are still the exception and are usually engraved. Of course, a good many invitations to grand functions, either business or purely social, are still being engraved, but the point is, no one will think the less of you if you have yours printed.

The lettering on engraved invitation cards should be copperplate. On printed cards it should be letterpress script. The lettering should be black, not silver or coloured, and the paper should be white, of good weight and quality. No doubt you have seen those cheerful cards on sale at the stationers. Such cards have deckle edges, may be printed in red, blue or any colour of the rainbow, and are gaily decorated with cocktail glasses, floating bubbles, horseshoes and just about anything else. Many of us enjoy using these cards, but it is as well to bear in mind that they are considered to be in bad taste, so when any of your husband's business contacts are involved, you would be wiser to stick to the traditional plain white card.

Your invitation card should indicate the day and month of the party, but not the year, e.g. Friday, July 2nd, is sufficient. O'clock is considered preferable to a.m. and p.m. Some people even like to quibble about whether R.S.V.P. should go in the bottom right-hand corner or in the opposite one. You would be well advised to let common sense settle this minor detail and put it on the right if there is room and on the left if the layout looks more balanced this way. And of course, R.S.V.P. stands for *répondez s'il vous plaît*, the French for 'please answer'. Whenever these initials appear on an invitation it is polite to reply as requested.

Strictly speaking, invitations should go out in your name only, as the hostess, and your name, c.g. Mrs John Brown should be hand written in the centre of the card. The guests' names should be hand written in the top left-hand corner of the card. Guests should be addressed as Mr George Smith, Miss Helen Doakes, Mr and Mrs Alan Greene, Lord and Lady Blank and so on, as the case may be. A doctor and his wife are addressed as Dr and Mrs A. B. White. A widow is addressed in the same way as she would be if her husband were alive, that is, Mrs Peter Brown. A divorced woman, on

the other hand, recovers her Christian name and is consequently addressed as Mrs Josephine Brown. When a man has
both a service rank and a title, usually only the title is used
on the card. This means that Admiral Sir Arthur and Lady
Winslow should be addressed as Sir Arthur and Lady Winslow. The prefix 'Hon.' or letters after names are not used on
invitation cards.

It is also useful to know that a great many invitations to
business functions do not give the guests' names at all, but an
engraved card simply 'requests the pleasure of your
company' to whatever the function may be.

The 'At Home' card is used for invitations to cocktail
parties, informal dinners, dances and almost any other kind
of reception, with the exception of weddings. You can have
'At Home' cards engraved with your name, R.S.V.P. and the
address on them, leaving only the remaining details to be
filled in by hand. When completed, such a card would look
like Fig. 2. Equally acceptable and less expensive are the

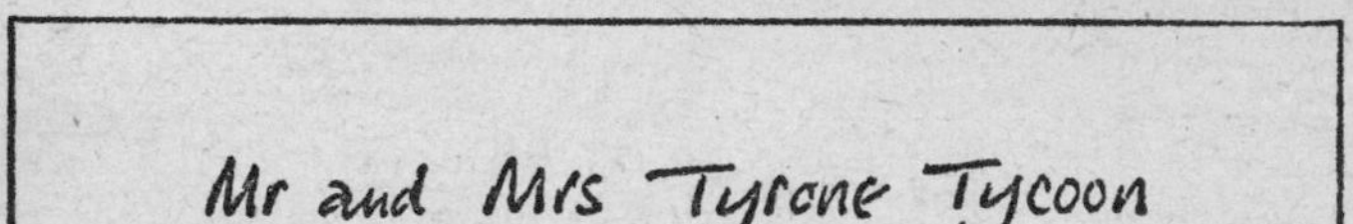

Mr and Mrs Tyrone Tycoon

Mrs Sydney Swank

At Home

Thursday July 1st

R.S.V.P.
23 Merrivale,
London, S.W.3

Cocktails
6 o'clock

Figure 2 'At Home' card with name of hostess engraved

cards which you can buy from any stationer with only 'At Home', 'Cocktails', and 'R.S.V.P.' printed or engraved on them (Fig. 3).

At Home

R.S.V.P.   *Cocktails*

Figure 3 A simpler 'At Home' card

For formal dinners, dances, and other functions, printed or engraved cards can be bought from the stationer or specially ordered for the occasion. As with 'At Home' cards, the ready-printed cards need to have the name of the hostess, as well as the address and details of the party filled in by hand. If it is to be an evening dress affair, then the words 'Black tie' go in the bottom left-hand corner of the card.

If a special card is being printed or engraved, it would look like Fig. 4 when properly filled in.

As we have seen in the case of a married couple, invitations should correctly go out in the name of the hostess only, but there is a trend towards both husband and wife appearing jointly on invitation cards. This new trend would seem particularly apt in cases where you are entertaining your husband's business associates, some of whom you may not even know. Another trend, particularly among younger couples, is to drop the Mr and Mrs, both from the names of host and hostess and from those of guests. This would give us John and Mary Brown inviting Michael and Carole White. Both these trends seem eminently sensible and more in keeping with our present way of life and you may well decide that this is the right formula for you.

Mrs Sydney Swank
requests the pleasure of
Mr and Mrs Tyrone Tycoon's

.*company at dinner on*
Wednesday, November 10th at 8 o'clock

The Firs
Winding Lane
Gerrards Cross
Buckinghamshire   *R.S.V.P.*

Figure 4 An example of a specially printed invitation to a formal dinner

While business invitations are sent to a person's business address, purely social invitations should be sent to a person's private address. In the case of a married couple, the envelope is addressed to the wife. Moreover the form of address differs in some instances between the card itself and the envelope. For instance, while the prefix 'Hon.' is not put on the invitation card, it does go on the envelope. In such cases 'Esquire' is omitted. So that in the case of a bachelor entitled to the 'Hon.' prefix, you should address the envelope to the Hon. David Greene.

If you are ever in doubt as to how to address any of your

husband's associates, it is always best to get on to the man's secretary, for she will always know the form, at any rate for her own boss and his wife.

Replying to formal invitations

People frequently get flustered when they receive one of those impressive-looking engraved invitations which address you as if you were a monument, in the third person. In point of fact there is one simple rule about answering invitations which makes the whole thing absurdly simple. This rule is: follow suit. In other words, if you receive an invitation from Mrs Sydney Snooty requesting the pleasure of the company of Mr and Mrs Tyrone Tycoon at dinner, you reply in the same vein. Your missive would read: 'Mr and Mrs Tyrone Tycoon thank Mrs Sydney Snooty for her kind invitation to dinner on such and such a date and are pleased to accept'.

Should your invitation follow the latest trend and omit the Mrs and Mr, then you do likewise. If the invitation is quite informal, then you just scribble your acceptance on an informal card. There is a very valid point in this business of following suit, since if your hostess is following a modern trend and you reply in the strictly conventional way, you would appear to be correcting her or even criticising her and showing her that you know better—and this, of course, is very bad manners.

In an ideal world all invitations are welcome and we are always free to accept them. In real life, however, it is not always so. Some events are a real ordeal, while some very delightful invitations find us already committed elsewhere. Yet some invitations simply cannot be turned down. Those from your man's superiors or from his clients or other business connections come under this heading most of the time. If his boss invites the two of you to dinner, you *could* get out of it if you had a very good reason, but on the whole you would do well to accept.

If you do have to turn down an invitation, it is polite to

give the reason, such as illness, absence abroad, previous engagement or whatever.

Write your reply, either by hand or on the typewriter, in the centre of the page, in one block, and let it stand alone, with neither date nor any further embellishment. Here is Tracy Tycoon turning down Sara Snooty:

> Mr and Mrs Tyrone Tycoon thank Mrs Sydney Snooty for her kind invitation to dinner on October 30, but regret that they are unable to accept owing to a previous engagement.

If you do accept, then you should repeat the date, time and place of the event to indicate that you have duly noted and understood them.

The only other point about replying to invitations, whether formal or informal, is that it is polite to reply as quickly as possible. Nothing is more infuriating to a hostess than to send out invitations and then be left in an agony of suspense for days on end wondering whether anyone is going to accept. So be a dear and reply right away.

Letter-writing

The next item in your social-secretary's kit is some good stationery. Select a good quality paper in either white, off-white, grey or pale blue, with matching envelopes. Do take the advice of a good stationer, as there is more to paper than meets the eye. As for size, it is a matter of personal taste, but 8 in. × 6 in. is a good size, or you might decide to have two different sizes to accommodate short and long letters.

An engraved address is, of course, the best solution, but failing that, then ordinary letterpress printing will have to do. Your address should either be centred at the top of the page, with the telephone number underneath, likewise centred, or it can be in the right-hand top corner, indented, with the telephone number across the opposite corner. Use a simple typeface. Upper case throughout is more usual than upper and lower case. Here again, ask your stationer's advice, if in doubt.

Deckle edges and coloured borders used to be considered in bad taste, but there is a trend now towards not only borders, but flowery script, special monograms and even little sketches of the writer's home. Do bear in mind, however, that a businessman's wife is not supposed to be a trend-setter and that your best bet is to lean in the direction of conventional good taste, without being stuffy about it, of course.

There also used to be many snobbish rules about envelope size and 'proper' flaps, but nowadays it is far more important to see that the envelopes you order conform to the Post Office preferred sizes, otherwise they will be delayed in the mail. If you decide on two sizes of writing paper, you can select an envelope which will take both, the smaller size folded once, perhaps, and the larger size folded twice. As mentioned previously the smallest P.O.P. envelope size is 5½ in. × 3⅜ in. The largest size is 9¼ in. × 4¾ in. Envelopes between these sizes should have the longer side 1·414 times the length of the shorter side.

Forms of address

You are now all set and equipped for letter-writing and the first thing for you to bear in mind here is that it is nowadays perfectly in order to typewrite personal letters of all sorts. A charming variation on the theme which adds a personal touch, is to 'top and tail' your letters, that is, to write in by hand the 'Dear Josephine' and the 'Yours sincerely'.

If you do a great deal of letter-writing, therefore, you will save time and your correspondents' eyesight if you equip yourself with your own personal typewriter.

You will certainly have occasion to write a business letter now and again, if only to complain about poor service or query a bill, so it is as well for you to bear in mind that nowadays 'Messrs' is no longer used and in addressing a company you simply write: Lloyds Bank Limited, Greene, White and Associates or whatever.

Strictly speaking, all business letters should be addressed to the company, but you will frequently get better attention if you address your letter personally to the man concerned with your particular business. In this case you would address your envelope to: Charles W. Smith, Esq., Sales Manager, followed by the company's name. More correct, but by no means always done, is to address your envelope to the company and then to write in the bottom left-hand corner, 'For the attention of Charles W. Smith, Esq.' If you have addressed your business letter to someone in particular, then you begin: 'Dear Mr Smith' and end 'Yours sincerely'. If you have addressed your letter to the company, then you begin: 'Dear Sirs', and end 'Yours faithfully'.

When it comes to personal letters, there is no problem at all: it is invariably 'Dear Mr So-and-So', 'Dear Mrs So-and-So', or 'Dear Miss So-and-So', ending with 'Yours sincerely', or for closer friends 'Dear Joe, Mary' or what have you, ending with 'Yours sincerely', 'As ever', or 'Love' for close friends.

As for addressing the envelope, there is usually very little trouble here. It is either: 'Mr and Mrs John Taylor', 'John W. Taylor, Esq.,' or 'Miss Muriel Hobbs'. Widows, divorcées and 'Hons' we have already dealt with. Suffixes denoting Masters' or Bachelors' degrees, M.A., B.A., B.Sc., are rarely used, except when writing to someone in the teaching profession.

Letters standing for membership of learned societies are usually added only if they imply special distinction. You should add F.R.S. (Fellow of the Royal Society), F.B.A. (Fellow of the British Academy), F.S.A. (Fellow of the Society of Antiquaries of London), R.A. (Royal Academician), A.R.A. (Associate of the Royal Academy), but not F.R.Hist.S. (Fellow of the Royal Historical Society) or F.R.G.S. (Fellow of the Royal Geographical Society).

All letters addressed to Members of Parliament should

have M.P. after the name. All letters addressed to Privy Councillors should have the prefix The Rt Hon. Members of Parliament who are also Privy Councillors get the full treatment, e.g. The Rt Hon. John Brown, M.P. Initials of all orders precede M.P., e.g. Sir John Brown, K.C.M.G., M.P. Dame Elizabeth Brown, D.B.E., M.P.

Initials indicating professional qualifications or official status should be used only for professional or official correspondence. This relieves you of quite a headache when attending to your social correspondence. There are only two exceptions to this rule: one is M.P., as we have seen, and the other is Q.C. (Queen's Counsel).

Honours initials should follow the name. Knights are addressed: Sir John Blank, if a Knight Bachelor, but otherwise followed by the initials of the appropriate order of chivalry. Wives of knights take the title 'Lady', followed by the husband's surname. Dames are addressed as Dame Mary Brown, followed by the initials of the appropriate order. In addressing a knight holding more than one degree in one or more orders of chivalry, show only the senior appointment in each order, e.g. G.C.V.O., and not G.C.V.O., K.C.V.O., C.V.O.

General practitioners and surgeons are both correctly addressed in the same way as ordinary mortals. However, physicians are frequently given the courtesy title of 'Doctor', whether they actually have an M.D. or not and it is perfectly in order to address them on an envelope as Dr F. R. Brown.

Clergymen are addressed: To the Rev. John Blank. Officers in the armed forces are addressed according to rank, giving either the full Christian name or initials, followed by the surname. For instance: Lieutenant-General C. B. Mathews; Air Commodore W. S. Lewis, R.A.F.; Group Officer Beryl Richards, W.R.A.F.

You will recall that where a man has both a service rank and a title, only the latter goes on the invitation card. When addressing the envelope, however, you give both, first the service rank, then the title. So our Admiral would be addressed on the envelope as Admiral Sir Arthur Winslow.

Sub-lieutenants, midshipmen, and cadets in the Royal Navy, lieutenants and second-lieutenants in the Army, and flying officers and pilot officers in the Royal Air Force are referred to as 'Mr' and therefore their letters should be addressed 'Esq.', followed by R.N., the name of their regiment, or R.A.F. respectively for each of the services. For instance: F. Brown, Esq., R.N., J. J. Jackson, Esq., Coldstream Guards, N. J. Watson, Esq., R.A.F. Decorations should be given after the name, e.g. Captain E. H. Dawson, D.S.O., R.N.

A British ambassador is addressed as follows: To His Excellency. Her Britannic Majesty's Ambassador Extraordinary and Plenipotentiary to ——— (name of country).

A British consul abroad is addressed: D. J. Wilkins, Esq., Consul to Her Britannic Majesty at ——— (name of country). Unless these gentlemen have a title, their wives are simply addressed as Mrs Douglas Wilkins or whatever.

A foreign ambassador to the Court of St James is addressed as follows: To His Excellency the Ambassador Extraordinary and Plenipotentiary of ——— (name of country he represents).

Should you need to address a letter to a member of the nobility, do not panic. Simply go to your nearest library and look up *Burke's Peerage, Baronetage and Knightage*. Indeed if you frequently write to such people and invite them to your home, you might do well to have Burke's always near at hand, as it will solve for you all your problems of precedence, which can be so worrying to the unwary.

Dropping a line

Some people get unnecessarily worried when the need arises to put pen to paper. They wonder what to say, fuss over grammar, and feel a need to put on an act. There is really no need for any of this. First of all, be yourself. Write as you speak. Don't attempt to be other than you are or to impress your correspondent with big words—it never works.

Secondly, letters are not meant to go on and on *ad infinitum.* Ask yourself: 'Why am I writing?'. If it is to say 'thank you', then say it, add a thoughtful sentence to show you have truly appreciated whatever it is you are saying 'thank you' for and sign off. If the letter is truly hard to write, as letters of condolence are, then look into your heart and ask yourself: 'What words would comfort me in such a situation? How would I feel in her place?' Feel with your correspondent, put yourself in his or her place and you cannot fail to think of the right words.

THANK-YOU LETTERS While it is by no means *de rigueur* and so few people do it, a hostess always appreciates a little note the day after the party. It makes all her efforts worthwhile and gives her a lift just when she is feeling the letdown which so frequently follows the strenuous efforts of entertaining. So do make a habit of writing a brief note to your hostess. Write, if at all possible, immediately you return home, then it will be done. Postponed until the following morning, it will remain a pious intention.

You might say something like this:

> Dear Mrs Greene,
>
> I should like to thank you most sincerely for a truly delightful evening, George and I enjoyed it immensely and I must say we were both tremendously impressed with the way you conjured up those *pêches flambés* right before our eyes!
>
> > Yours sincerely,
> > Jean Miller

If the hostess did not do her own cooking, then you don't praise the cuisine, but mention the special decorations, if any, or the magnificent position of the home, if it was your first visit, or how much you enjoyed meeting one of the other guests. In other words, think of some aspect of the evening which you particularly enjoyed and say a couple of gracious words about it. It is just as simple as that. If you have spent a week-end or even only one night at someone's home, then a 'bread-and-butter' letter is an absolute 'must', but there is no need to say any more. Obviously if there was a ball, or a hunt or some special event, you also say how much you enjoyed that.

THE NOTE OF APOLOGY   It sometimes happens that a few lines of apology are called for. If you break anything while a guest in someone's home, apologise briefly, but without causing a fuss, and if the broken item is replaceable, send it along with a short note, reiterating your apologies. If the item is irreplaceable, then the least you can do is send along some flowers and a note.

You might say:

> Dear Mrs Fuller,
>   I should like you to know how very distressed I am for damaging your Ming vase last night, the more so in that the damage cannot be undone, nor the vase replaced.
>   Perhaps these flowers will tell you better than I can in words just how sorry I am.
>
>   Yours sincerely,
>   Muriel Manning

THE LETTER OF INTRODUCTION   When travelling abroad, especially alone, there is nothing more useful than an introduction to someone who can help you to see the sights, introduce you to people you want to meet or help you with shopping. So if a friend is in this situation and you can help her out with an introduction, then by all means do so. Such letters are simplicity itself to write. Just say who the traveller is, what she plans to do on her trip and what services she is likely to be in need of. It is also useful to add a word about what the two people have in common, if anything.

It might very well be, however, that your departing

friend, though perfectly charming in all other respects, has an Achilles heel which it is only fair for your correspondent to be warned about. There is no reason why this should present complications, however. You must frankly warn your correspondent, in the nicest possible way, and, of course, don't give a carbon of your letter to your departing friend!

You could say:

> Dear Gertrude,
>
> A college friend of mine, Sally Weaver, is about to take off on a solo trip to Italy and since she speaks not a word of Italian and this is her first trip abroad, I promised to write to you and tell you to expect a call from her.
>
> If she does call, do be nice to her and show her around a bit. She is purely on a pleasure bent and will want to visit the art galleries and churches and would no doubt enjoy a drive up to Fiesole and that sort of thing.
>
> I'm sure you will enjoy Sally's company. She is a very lively girl and an amusing conversationalist. I do feel in duty bound, however, to give you the gypsy's warning on one small point. Sally is a bit of a *femme fatale* and considers any man who strikes her fancy as fair game. So I'd advise you to take her around during the day time, when you're on your own, and introduce her to some nice young man you have no designs on yourself.
>
> Thanks a million and let me know if Sally calls and how you get along together.
>
> > Sincerely,
> > Joan

LETTERS OF CONDOLENCE   These are perhaps the most difficult letters to write. It is best to make them quite brief, since once you have conveyed the idea that you feel for the bereaved person, additional words can do nothing to alleviate the pain.

Let simplicity and sincerity be your guide and you cannot go wrong. Just say your piece and be done. Long philosophical messages on the meaning of life and death, detailed dwelling on the virtues and attributes of the departed only serve to rub salt into the wound. By all means pay a suitable tribute to the deceased person, but resist the temptation to go on and on.

It is best to write such messages right away, otherwise they tend to be put off indefinitely. Obviously, you will want to tailor your letter according to your degree of friendship for the bereaved person, the known feelings between the person who has died and the one left behind, and the temperament and other characteristics of your correspondent.

Here is one example, by no means to be copied slavishly for all occasions:

> Dear Mrs White,
> Even though mere words can do little to comfort you at a time such as this, I want you to know how much I sympathise with you in your bereavement. May the kind thoughts and sympathy of your friends help to give you courage and fortitude.
>
> Yours sincerely,
> Hellen Wallis

CHAPTER SIX

CONTACTS WITH THE COMPANY

Everything we have talked about so far could be described as working behind the scenes. When you come into contact with the people your man works with you are well and truly on stage. When you do this everything must be in place: costume impeccable, make-up in order, lines off pat. The only thing you will have no control over is the lighting! If you think of your role in terms of playing a part, not only will you have hit upon the truth of the matter, but it will help you to be aware of yourself and to do the right thing even if it does not particularly appeal to you. So turn on your smile and make your entrance.

As you may have noticed, we are living in transitional times. Never before has the world changed at such a dizzy speed. This situation makes life very difficult for us, the inhabitants of this agitated planet. For some, the very old, it makes life no longer bearable. For others it means additional stress and strain because we can no longer be sure of what is the right thing to do in this or that circumstance. Such things used to be handed down from parents to children. Books could be written telling the uninitiated just what to wear for this or that occasion; how to behave, what to say, what to do, what to avoid.

Now it is no longer so. No sooner has one authority decided that it is now in order to relax Ruling No. 1 than the public at large relaxes Rulings No. 2, 3 and 4. So what is the thoughtful person to do? Unquestionably, it requires a great deal more self-assurance, a great deal more self-discipline and a great deal more inner strength to do the right thing these days.

And so, you, the conscientious wife anxious to further her man's career, must extend your extra-sensory antennae to their utmost, use your powers of observation and your feminine intuition to *feel* your way into doing exactly the right thing when you step on that stage and say your piece before your husband's colleagues, his superiors and, indeed, his staff.

The first thing you will need to find out—and your husband will help you here, of course—is just what kind of company it is your man is working for, that is, are they hidebound conservatives, way out futurists or which stage in between. Every company has a style and you must discover what this style is and then follow suit. In essence it is just as simple as that.

It is simple enough to discover at which end of the pole the company is situated. The very nature of the business will tell you this and indeed you have only to ask your husband. As a rule of thumb, however, you can be sure that banks, insurance companies, stockbrokerage houses and other financial institutions, learned societies and, of course, the Government, occupy the most conservative side of the spectrum. Organisations dealing with more creative activities—and the term is used very loosely indeed—are apt to be at the other extreme. Your man's company obviously fits somewhere between these two extremes and the man, or men, at the top will set the 'tone'. If you find out exactly what this 'tone' is and follow suit as if to the manner born you will be an inestimable asset to your husband and worth your weight in gold!

His secretary and you

If your husband does a lot of business entertaining you will have a lot to do with his secretary. In any event you would do well to consider her your greatest ally in this business of furthering your man's career, for that is indeed what she is doing, with none of the frills which you enjoy.

In dealing with your husband's secretary, you will at once dispel from your mind any notion of jealousy or fear that you might have in her a rival. It would be foolish indeed of you to entertain such thoughts. There no doubt are a few secretaries who have affairs with their boss, but by and large women who habitually have affairs with married men choose easier jobs. The secretary's job is an exacting one and unless you still have confetti in your hair you will realise that that precious man of yours is not unalloyed joy to be with all day. In fact you can be sure the poor girl has quite a bit to put up with, so it would be grossly unfair of you to be jealous of her to boot.

So there she is, your man's closest associate who knows him at least as well as you do yourself. Be friendly with her and *never* adopt a superior attitude. Resist the temptation of quizzing her on business matters or on your husband's moves. If she is a good secretary she will evade your questions in any event, so it is more dignified to withold the questions.

Do not be tempted to hand over to your husband's secretary certain chores which you should do yourself, such as checking your bank account. When it comes to company affairs or other events which you are to attend with your man, then work closely with his secretary, making sure you enter times and dates in the various diaries and do not get them mixed up. All in all, dealing with your husband's secretary should be perfectly simple and straightforward, for with her you can afford to be yourself and do not need to mind your p's and q's so much. If you treat her in a friendly and appreciative manner she will be just as helpful to you, in those few dealings you have with her, as she is to your husband.

You will be wise to extend the relationship no further and in no event should you attempt to make a confidante of her. That is not her role and you must seek such solace elsewhere.

Apart from your husband's secretary, you will no doubt at times come into contact with other members of his staff: assistants, typists, charge-hands, office boys, apprentices, gardeners, drivers—anyone in fact who reports to him. With such people it is simply a question of being gracious, remembering to say 'Good morning' and 'thank you' when the need arises and making it clear that you do indeed know they are alive and have a friendly feeling towards them. Nothing could be simpler and nothing is more frequently neglected. It is very instructive to note that the truly 'great' never neglect this kind of graciousness.

Your husband's colleagues

On the surface your husband's colleagues will appear to be nice ordinary chaps, or perhaps rather dull ones and, once in a while, one of them might appear to be rather attractive, dashing, brilliant or any other attribute you care to think of. Behind this surface, however, you would be wise to bear in mind that envy, rivalry, suspicion and inquisitiveness may lurk, and probably do.

This is only human, for a colleague is not simply a friend. A colleague works for the same company, may be competing for the same position higher up the ladder, may be trying to 'sell' a different approach to the company chairman, and is almost certainly trying to outshine your man in order to further his career. In other words, you must face the fact that in the rat race all the rats are rivals, not brethren.

This being the hard, naked fact, you cannot afford simply to sit back and relax while entertaining your man's colleague and his lady in your home. You must go right on playing that role and your role is that of the charming, attentive hostess who never drops her guard for a single minute.

If the men could simply avoid talking 'shop' altogether, you'd be home and dry, but unfortunately two men from the same company can scarcely refrain from doing so, and the advice to refrain would be a counsel of perfection. However, it should be borne in mind that it would be extremely ill-mannered in the event of a foursome dinner for the two men to go on and on about the business and leave the women folk to their own devices. Yet a great many of such rude men do exist.

So while the men are talking business, leave them to it and don't butt in with a bit of advice of your own and don't 'kibitz', as they say in the States. There *are* exceptions to this rule, for very often your opinion, representing that of a consumer, could be most valuable. If for instance the men are having a very informal discussion on the new spring line or new colours, they may very well seek your preferences and opinions. In fact, businessmen with teen-age children not infrequently ask them and their friends for their opinion on items for young people they are manufacturing or marketing.

So do give your opinion when asked. Otherwise leave them to it and hope they'll have the good grace to change the subject before the evening grows too dull. When you have the colleague to yourself do refrain from prying into business matters and conversely play dumb if he should start 'pumping' you. Never be tempted to criticise the company they both work for, or the boss, the other executives in the company and above all, of course, your own man. Neither should you repeat anything which you have been told in confidence, however tempted to do so you may be. It may sound like a highly unnecessary piece of advice, but some men are highly skilful at securing the information they want and do not hesitate to use all the charm they are capable of to this end. So beware, especially of that attractive one.

As for the wives of colleagues, you would be well advised here too to stick to any subject except your husbands' business. It is so tempting to let your hair down with another woman, but it can be dynamite if she happens to be the wife of your man's colleague. So stick to the birds and bees, your pet projects, the theatre, books, anything, in fact except 'the works'. If the dear lady tries to probe, fend her off.

If all this sounds rather like jungle warfare, it is not really meant to be. It simply means that in dealing with your husband's colleagues you will need a great deal of self-discipline. Once you have trained yourself not to discuss certain subjects and not to divulge certain information, then you can relax and enjoy the company of the people with whom your man has so much in common. The marching orders are: keep your hair pinned well up all the time!

The boss

You will hardly need reminding that your man's career will be greatly influenced by his boss. This can come about in a number of ways, not only in the sense that the boss is the man who hands out the rises and promotions. It is far more complex and far more important than that. One of the executive's most important tasks is the development of his subordinates. It is his business to know each one of them, their capabilities and weaknesses, potentialities and ambitions and to help them to grow and achieve these potentialities. It follows that there is absolutely nothing more important for a man than to find himself a good boss, for nothing can help him to grow more than working for the right man, a man who knows and accepts his responsibilities as a builder of men. To work for a man of calibre is a privilege indeed and all too few people enjoy this privilege.

When an executive is considering accepting a position he should not be asking himself: 'What is the salary?', but 'What is the calibre of the man I shall be reporting to?' If the boss is right, then the battle will be half won.

If your husband is fortunate enough to report to a man of this calibre, you both have a great deal to be thankful for.

The boss will be interested in meeting you. He will want to form an opinion as to whether there is harmony in the home and whether you are behind your man and want to see him get ahead or whether on the contrary you keep on nagging him to get into something more relaxed and leave the rat race to others.

Ultimately if you have something serious to conceal, such as dissent within your marriage, there is nothing you can really do to hide it, for dissimulate as you will, the sensitive person will sense the tension between you. If, on the other hand, you are a happy pair this too will come across. So that ultimately you must simply be yourself and make not the slightest attempt to put on an act of any sort.

You are still playing businessman's wife, of course, but you are not deliberately playing happy couple or anything like that. See the subtle difference? So make sure you are well-turned out, be friendly, alert, listen well, don't talk too much, and, of course, make the dear man comfortable if you are entertaining him.

Other than this, the same rules apply as with colleagues. Don't discuss their business unless asked, don't pry, and don't be foolish enough to try to influence the boss in your man's favour. He will see through this instantly and it is quite unnecessary if both men are the right kind of men!

Some British companies nowadays follow the practice of interviewing the wife too when seeking a new executive on the open market. Likewise, when a man is being considered for promotion, especially if it is planned to send him abroad, the wife is sometimes asked to go along and talk it over. Sometimes these interviews take on a social flavour and are not nearly so awesome as they sound.

If you should be faced with such a situation, don't panic. There's absolutely nothing to worry about. All the boss really wants to know is (1) are you happy about the prospect of taking your family to Argentina for a three-year spell, or (2) will you be able to cope with all the business entertaining which will come your way in the important new job he is cooking up for your man, or (3) how will you feel about your man being away from home most weeks, sometimes for days at a stretch? or (4) would you be happy to leave London or go to London or live in a small town or whatever the case may be, or (5) is your marriage such a ruin that your man will be too emotionally upset to attend to his job properly.

Although many people strongly object to these efforts to find out how a wife feels about such things, it is really only reasonable, since a great deal of time and money is invested in an executive and it would be foolish indeed to send him off to the new branch in Argentina or Timbuctoo if his wife is dead against it. Moreover, it is fairer to the wife to give her a chance of upsetting the apple car with one fell swoop. You must realise that you have the opportunity to do this and if your man has been trying to coerce you into agreeing to go off to Scotland, Outer Mongolia or New Guinea and the very thought appals you, then you have every right to let the chairman know in no uncertain terms. After all, you should be taken into consideration too, and this is just what the company wants to do, for its own sake, admittedly, but the company's reasons in this particular case, in any event, coincide perfectly with your own personal interests.

View the meeting with the Big Man in this light and you're home and dry. If you're really and truly in favour of the promotion, then make enthusiastic noises: 'Oh, I'd be delighted if Bob were given the job in Argentina. I took Spanish at evening classes a long time ago, so I'd soon get into the swing of the language.' Or: 'I've always thought I'd like to live abroad and I think it'd be good for the children, too. If there's time I could start learning the language before we leave.' Or: 'I'd really welcome an opportunity of entertaining more. I learned so many exciting dishes at the Cordon Bleu School, but so seldom have an opportunity to try them out.' And so on. The idea is to show either that you have already been doing a little bit of what it is you'd be called upon to do, or demonstrate your willingness to learn what is necessary and, above all, your awareness of what would be involved.

If it were a question of going abroad, for instance, you would need to demonstrate your willingness to begin learning the language, your adaptability, your capacity for making new friends and adjusting to a new way of life and if you have a family, your conviction that a stay abroad would be equally good for them.

If it were a question of your moving into 'higher social spheres', so to speak, then you must let the Big Man decide for himself. There would be no point in putting on any airs and graces, or worse yet, a 'posh' accent. If you do anything like this the result can only be dismal failure. Bear in mind that wise people judge others for what they are, not according to their accent or family background. So be your own charming self and hope for the best.

If the job or promotion your man is hoping for would involve long absences from the home, then you must demonstrate your self-sufficiency, show that you have a number of hobbies and friends which will occupy your time. Convey the idea that while you would, of course, prefer to see more of your man, you realise how important this new opportunity is and would not like him to miss out on it. If you do *not* believe a word of this, then for goodnes sake tell your man fairly and squarely and if he will not listen, then upset the apple cart for him and let the boss know exactly how you feel. *That* will fix it. You must exercise what little power you have, you know!

The only other point to bear in mind in this interview situation is not to wax over-anxious. Don't oversay your piece. Don't gush. Don't blabber on and on. Be poised, smiling, relaxed, self-controlled, self-assured and you'll have the Old Man reaching for the First Prize rosette.

Company functions

There will be times when you will be able to enjoy *all* the pleasures outlined in this chapter at one fell swoop. Such an occasion is the company function: annual dinner, office party, ladies' night or what-have-you.

Some would view such occasions as a masochist's delight, but there really is no reason to take this view. While you could persuade yourself that you were going to have to cope not only with your man's secretary or his favourite colleague, but with all his colleagues, *and* their wives, *and* the boss, *and* his wife, plus perhaps even other guests. Oh, dearie me. In point of fact, you won't be on exhibition. Everyone will be so concerned with themselves that they will hardly notice how you look, what you say or how you behave. Is this crushing? It is true, none the less.

So just follow the same 'rules' previously outlined and make up your mind to have a good time. Your invitation will tell you whether it's a dress affair or an informal 'do'. Bearing in mind what we said about company style, if in doubt, lean more towards the conservative than the revolutionary in dress and you won't go far wrong. Another good dodge is to notice what every other woman is wearing and next time make sure you are wearing something reasonably similar, at least in flavour.

So much, then for dress. With a bit of luck, there will not be too much business talk at the party, so you will not be tempted to tell them how to run the company. Otherwise the field is wide open: discuss whatever you like, except your operation. Go easy with religion and politics, for while not really taboo subjects any longer, in business it is wiser to keep your thoughts to yourself on these matters. Better also refrain from telling blue jokes.

Do not seize the opportunity to buttonhole the boss and give him a piece of your mind. This is definitely not done. Charm him rather by your graciousness and by being a good listener. Office functions are not intended for airing grie-

vances and bringing up the subject of overdue rises and so on.
They are intended to stress the fact that the company is one
big happy family and you will not be thanked if you do not
play the game.

Needless to say, you will avoid having too much to drink
and you will keep your flirting at the most harmless level.
These two points are not only obvious ones, but very important ones indeed.

There are company functions at which you will be expected to do a little more than just have a good time. You
may, in fact, be called upon to say the proverbial 'few
words'. There is no reason why this should dismay you as we
shall see in the chapter which follows.

CHAPTER SEVEN

SAYING 'A FEW WORDS'

Whether to give a vote of thanks on a ladies' night or in chairing a committee of your Townswomen's Guild, sooner or later you will find yourself having to say the proverbial 'few words'. And whether the occasion is one of your husband's functions or a hobby of your own you will want to acquit yourself well. Indeed, there is no need to panic, for thousands of women, all over the world, are delivering excellent speeches every day of the year. Conversely, there are any number of men who speak very badly indeed. So, you see, it is not a matter of whether one is male or female, but of mastering the art of public speaking.

The secret of success is organisation and preparation and this is not to be understood as two big words, but to be taken absolutely literally. It is quite amazing how many people presume to stand up before a gathering and deliver a talk, or even give a short report, without the slightest preparation. Then they wonder why they made such a wretched job of it.

Even more important than organisation and preparation, is sincerity. Without it no one can hope to succeed as a speaker, yet unlike organisation and preparation, it is not there for the asking. You cannot tell anyone to be sincere. People either are or they are not. And you cannot hope to fool people, for everyone recognises falseness and hypocrisy, while sincerity never fails to make its presence felt. It shines through every word that is said.

Do not worry if you are a shy person, for some experts maintain that shy people make excellent public speakers. There once was a professor of English who actually blushed when speaking to a girl pupil individually, yet when he stood up before the whole class he gave some truly magnificent and inspiring lectures.

So rest assured that if you have something to say, if you sincerely believe in what you have to say, if you organise your talk well and rehearse it thoroughly you cannot fail as a speaker, whether you plan simply to propose a vote of thanks or to deliver a lengthy talk.

The parts of a speech

A talk, like a letter, should have a beginning, a middle and an end. It should flow logically from A to B to C, carrying the audience along with it. The logical progression is as follows:

1 THE CLARION CALL This serves to wake the audience up and gain its attention. You might call it the heigh-ho, since in effect it says: 'Heigh-ho there, listen to me.' It is a vital part of your talk, since if you do not have your audience's attention you might just as well save your breath.

2 THE PROPOSITION At this point you state your case.

3 THE EVIDENCE Now you bring in your facts and figures to prove your case.

4 THE CONCLUSION Here you show what conclusions can be drawn from the facts you have presented.

5 THE 'SO WHAT' Now you tell your audience what you want them to do about it.

Not every speech need contain all these parts, of course,

but keep them in mind as you write your talk down, so that you only leave out a part if it really is not needed.

How to begin

Making a start is always the hardest part, whether it be making a speech, writing a letter or indeed beginning any new project. With talks it is almost always necessary to wake the audience up, sometimes quite literally, so the 'Heigh-ho' is very important indeed.

First of all, if you are daring enough to start off by saying: 'Hallo everybody', as you wave a cheery hand, so much the better. Some people will be shocked and that is *bound* to wake them up. No doubt, however, you will want to shelter behind the conventional 'Ladies and Gentlemen' and let them sleep on until you arouse them with your next sentence. There are many ways you can begin and the method you choose will depend on your personality, the occasion and the type of talk you are giving. Here are some suggestions:

1 THE COMPLIMENT   Say how happy you are to be there, or how delighted you are to meet them all at last, or to meet them all again, or whatever the case may be. This is an excellent opening, since it pleases your audience and you're starting off on the right foot by referring to *them*, the most important subject in their eyes.

2 THE JOKE   This is a very common form of opening, but it is not so easy to handle and is perhaps not very suitable for a woman, but, of course, if humour is your *forte*, then by all means use this type of opening.

3 THE STORY   This is very similar to the joke opening, except that it is not a joke! We all love a story and providing it is relevant to your theme, by all means use the story opening. But make it a brief story.

4 THE STARTLING FACT   This is an excellent attention getter and is suitable for a fund-raising speech or one which aims at making converts.

5 THE QUOTATION   Here you start off by quoting one of the classics, a witty quip, a well-known personality, or a previous speaker, as appropriate. This type of opening is, of course, excellent in the case of literary talks, but not very suitable for a gathering of businessmen, even on a ladies' night.

6 CHRISTMAS AGAIN   This is a suitable opening for the kind of talk which takes place regularly every year, for instance at an annual meeting of a club or other institution when the activities of the past year are reviewed. If you are not careful, however, this type of opening can be rather dull.

7 THE APPEAL TO SELF-INTEREST   This is a useful opening gambit if your talk aims at 'selling' something, whether it be an idea or an actual commodity or service. However, unless you are a persistent reformer, you will probably find little use for this type of opening.

8 THE VISUAL AID   Some very successful speakers start right off with a visual aid, which they thrust at their audience from the word 'go'. You might hold up a rag doll and ask your audience: 'Can you guess who made this charming little doll?' You look over your audience smiling and after a good long pause you go on: 'A 21-year old girl with neither arms nor legs'—and you're off on your campaign to raise funds for the home for the handicapped.

9 THE GIMMICK   Here you walk on to the platform carrying some large object, doing something odd or otherwise creating a stir. Then you casually ask: 'I suppose you're wondering why I'm standing on my head?' Or: 'I suppose you're wondering what this curious

object is? Or: 'Why I'm wearing this huge pair of rose-tinted spectacles?' Then you go on to explain why or what it's all about. This is a tremendous opening, providing the gimmick is relevant to the subject. You probably won't have the courage to try it, alas.

Other ingredients of the successful speech

Having got your opening right, what else can you do to make your talk a success? Here are some pointers:

USE THE 'YOU' APPROACH   This means writing your speech from your audience's point of view. What is there in it for them? Think of your material from this point of view and cast your talk accordingly. Cut down on your 'I's and 'We's and insert plenty of 'You's instead. Don't say: 'I'm happy to tell you', but 'You'll be happy to learn.'

BE POSITIVE   You will not inspire your audience by telling them how unworthy you are to speak to them, how little time you had to prepare or that you left your notes behind. By no means say that this is the very first time you have made a speech, if this should be so. Try to feel confident and exude confidence. Always remember to accent the positive.

SHOW ENTHUSIASM   Enthusiasm is catching. If you really believe in your subject, let the audience see it. Nothing is more stimulating and more endearing than enthusiasm.

MAKE USE OF VISUAL AIDS The importance of visual aids in holding an audience's attention cannot be overstressed. Luckily there is scarcely a subject that cannot be brought home more clearly with illustrations, relevant objects or other visual aids. Even writing something on a blackboard is better than nothing.

STRIVE FOR AUDIENCE PARTICIPATION Nothing is more likely to keep your audience attentive than giving them something to do. If you are asking for a reply, it is worth alerting a friend in the audience beforehand to get the ball rolling. When one person replies, then the others will follow. If you can get your audience participating you can almost be sure that your talk will be a success.

Preparing the talk

This is where your advance preparation begins in earnest. There are, of course, several ways of preparing a speech, but for your particular purposes the very best method is the following: write down your entire talk, word for word, just as you intend to say it. Read it out aloud, preferably twice, then put the sheets away and write out on small cards the main points of your talk, in chronological order, only one or two points to the card. Write in a large bold hand and make each point succinctly. If you forget what the next point is, take a look at your notes, then continue again from memory.

When you have gone through the whole speech in this way, number your cards consecutively in large red numbers at the top right-hand corner. Now try making your speech by looking only at the cue-cards. Every time you fall by the wayside, look back on your previous notes. Correct yourself and go on. If you find you are forgetting a point, this means it should have gone on the cards in the appropriate place, so add it in. Keep on rehearsing your talk until you can give it without hesitation from the cue cards alone. Now tear up your original notes, stand up and deliver your talk, speaking aloud to the wall opposite. Keep on rehearsing until the day of the talk, then take your cue-cards with you, place them before you on lectern or table and use them without the slightest compunction. You will make a tremendous speech.

Delivery

Obviously, you will have presented yourself to the speaker's platform impeccably groomed. Not only will this give *you* added confidence, but it will inspire confidence in your audience.

Address yourself to the people in the last row of the auditorium. This will give you a better chance of being heard. If a microphone is provided, make sure you have an opportunity of trying it out before-hand. In fact, you should ask about this and the size of your audience before agreeing to talk in the first place.

Enunciate your words clearly, without slurring or hurrying. Try to look cheerful and smile as you approach the platform. Above all, look at your audience as you speak. Eye-contact with your audience is just about the most important aspect of delivery.

Try this plan: approach the platform with a smile, or if you are sitting on a rostrum or at a table, rise with a smile. Look your audience straight in the eye, as you let your gaze wander over from one side of the auditorium to the other. Continue to smile at them and then begin. Direct your talk first at the back row, then shift your gaze further forward, to the right and to the left and continue to maintain your eye-contact all the way through your talk.

Mannerisms to avoid

Nothing is more irksome to an audience than a speaker who is constantly humming and ha-ing, patting her hair, playing with her necklace or otherwise fidgeting. Such antics detract from what you are saying. In fact it is quite possible to become so fascinated by a speaker's antics as to miss entirely what he is trying to say.

So do try to be serene and poised while you talk. Your arms should be in repose as you begin. For some reason this appears to be the hardest thing to do—just to stand erect and let your arms hang relaxed by your side. It requires a little self-control, but it is well worth trying, for a speaker standing that way gives a strong impression of self-confidence. Gradually, as you warm to your subject, your arms and hands will move of their own accord to emphasise a point here, hold up a visual aid there, jot something on the blackboard. So try not to worry about your arms. They will take care of themselves, but do command your hands to be still, if they need it.

What to say

Strictly speaking, if you don't know what to say you have no business making a speech. In practice, however, there are several formal occasions when it is customary to say 'a few words' without there really being anything much to communicate. You might have occasion, in other words, of making a ritual speech. Such talks include official openings of bazaars, flower shows or exhibitions, prize-givings at schools or elsewhere, 'thank you' speeches of all sorts, introducing a speaker, accepting an office and after-dinner speeches.

Such talks call for sincerity, simplicity, courtesy and generosity. Brevity is also appreciated. A good plan to follow for such talks is to go from the general to the particular. In opening a bazaar, for instance, you might begin by saying something pleasant about the particular charity involved and then go on to dwell on the co-operation and teamwork which has made the bazaar possible. Here are some further suggestions.

INTRODUCING A SPEAKER Begin with a word of welcome to the speaker. Go on to say why he or she is especially well qualified to speak on the subject and end with: 'Ladies and Gentlemen, Mr John Spooner.' Above all, make it brief. Don't steal your speaker's thunder by anticipating what he is going to say. He won't thank you for it.

PROPOSING A VOTE OF THANKS   You can make this very brief indeed and simply say that you are delighted to propose a vote of thanks to Mr Spooner for his most interesting talk. There are occasions, however, when it would be courteous to say a little more. If the occasion is a school concert or amateur performance of some sort, it is thoughtful to say how excellent the performance was, how much you and the rest of the audience enjoyed it and to thank everyone for the hard work they put into it. You can end by wishing the Dramatic Society—or what-have-you— every success in the future or by saying how very much you and the rest of the audience appreciated their efforts.

AFTER-DINNER SPEECHES   Women are most fortunate in one respect and that is that they are not frequently called upon to make after-dinner speeches. The after-dinner speech is no easy task, particularly if impromptu. On most occasions at official dinners, all you will be required to do is rise after a toast has been proposed, raise your glass, repeat the words 'The Queen' or whatever the toast is, then take a genteel swig at the wine.

There is one occasion, however, which might call for a 'few words' and this is ladies' night. On such occasions one of the ladies, as agreed beforehand, usually says 'thanks for the party' on behalf of all the others. Bear in mind that the toast 'The Ladies', usually proposed by the youngest bachelor present, does not call for a reply, but ladies' nights are another matter.

Lots of women seem to make a bit of a hash of this simple little ritual and most of them are scared stiff if called upon to propose the vote of thanks. Many women make the mistake of going on and on and on—as indeed do men on similar occasions. Other women make the grotesque mistake of imitating their husband and sounding off about what a splendid company it is and how they must all pull together to make Nineteenseventyblank an even more successful year than the last!

It is really far simpler. All you are required to do is to say you would like to thank the chairman and directors (or whoever is responsible) on behalf of all the ladies present for a most enjoyable evening. If some special gesture has been made, then mention that: 'We were especially touched to receive the charming bouquets as we arrived' and so on. If the party is held in some specially interesting place, you might mention something about that, not so much generally, but picking out something specific. Obviously, if some special food is involved or has been specially flown in from Outer Mongolia, or something, then you will want to single it out for appreciation. If some special entertainment has been provided with you lassies in mind, then that too must come in for proper appreciation.

In short, it is simply a question of graciously appreciating what has been laid on on your behalf. Say something about the pleasure of seeing all those present and you're home and dry. But do say it all briefly. The best speech is the short speech.

CHAPTER EIGHT

ENTERTAINING

An accomplished hostess is of inestimable value to an ambitious man, be he in business, in politics, the diplomatic service or a score of other occupations. In fact it is no exaggeration to say that quite a number of women have actually made their husband's career by their *savoir faire* in captivating and entertaining the right people.

Of course, not every businessman needs to entertain his business contacts in the home and your hostessing may well be limited to having the occasional couple to dinner and once in a while receiving your man's boss and his lady. On the other hand, your home may well have a constant stream of visitors from abroad or clients and other contacts may have to be entertained quite frequently.

Only practice can make you that accomplished hostess which you aspire to be and even before practice, you need knowledge, knowledge of what to do and how to do it. If, therefore, you are a complete greenhorn in matters of cooking, you would be well advised to take one of the many courses now available, for gone are the days when the English hostess could get away with serving up dreary, monotonous, overcooked food or could opt out of even trying by having a professional cook to do the work for her. Nowadays every young woman is expected to turn out a well prepared and imaginative meal.

Opportunities for learning abound. If you live in London

you could do no better than to go along to the Cordon Bleu school. If Surrey is more convenient for you try the Tante Marie School of Cookery at Woking. Otherwise try your local college or one of the evening classes. You will find Continental cooking being taught almost everywhere now, but do make sure what the course is and who is teaching it before you sign up. You might even be able to take a wine course locally, for unbelievably enough, even colleges out of London are offering such courses in the evenings.

If you really cannot get away to a course, then take the Cordon Bleu part work on sale at most newsagents in 72 weekly instalments. Equally good, though somewhat different in approach is the Craddock Cookery Programme, also available in weekly instalments. This latter will also teach you something about wine, that indispensable accompaniment to good food.

Whatever you decide to do, make it a continuing and consistent effort, for it takes time and practice to become an accomplished cook and if your present level stretches no further than toad in the hole, it will be useless to go to one demonstration or to read the occasional recipe in the womens' magazines. If you have time you would also benefit from a course on flower arranging and these too are now available even in the smallest village. Once again, do take a whole course, for if you are a novice a single demonstration, while hugely entertaining, does not usually serve any lasting purpose.

Getting help

There are in fact three ways in which you can cope with entertaining. The first way is to hand over the whole mess to an outside caterer and leave yourself with nothing to do but receive your guests and play gracious hostess. One managing director, recently retired, acquired a great and perhaps undeserved reputation as a host by entertaining not only prospective clients, but the whole of his sales force in the great hall of his converted barn. All of the work was done by an outside caterer and he and his wife played lord and lady of the manor to the delight of the assembled company.

In recent years a new type of outside caterer has arisen: the skilful woman who runs her own catering business with no other help than one or two other women. These teams will come into your home and work in your kitchen just as if they were on your staff. You just tell them what food you want, how many people you are expecting and at what time and they come in and prepare everything for you, leaving you free to take care of the other details. Read the small ads in your local paper or inquire locally if you want to unearth one of these treasures.

The second way of coping is to do all your own cooking, but hire staff to help you on the night. This too is a great help. If your cooking is not yet up to scratch you might consider starting out with the little woman and later on taking your place in the kitchen and having staff come in to do the serving.

The third way is, alas, the most frequently met way these days. It involves doing the whole thing yourself, being what is called a cook-hostess, no mean feat. It can be done, of course, with planning and practice, but should not be attempted if you are having more than six people to dinner, eight including you and your man.

The drinks party

There is no need to plunge right into a large dinner party, however. Try a drinking party first, they are far easier to cope with and far less terrifying even for the novice. They are also far less costly than parties at which food is served. Some businessmen who have no expense account, such as for instance the owner-manager of a small company, find the drinks party a very useful and inexpensive way of entertaining their prospective clients just before Christmas without giving the slightest impression of being short of cash. One management consultant who badly needed rich clients did just this. He did not serve whisky and gin, of course, but mulled and spiced wine with half a bottle of vodka added. This concoction he prepared himself, presiding importantly over the steaming cauldron. Guests were tremendously impressed and the exchequer remained unscathed.

YOUR GUEST LIST   If you are giving the party for business reasons on behalf of your husband, then he will obviously let you have a list of people to invite and on some occasions it may even be a stag affair held rather early in the evening. If it is to be a sort of mixture twix business and pleasure, then wives will also be asked and you should also take the precaution of inviting two or three lively friends you can count on to keep the party going, otherwise you will find all the men huddled together talking business while the womenfolk get bored to tears.

In fact you would be wise not to expect a great deal of pleasure out of these cocktail parties with business overtones, because businessmen very seldom remember their social obligations on such occasions and insist on talking business the whole of the time.

If your guest list is a short one, then you will issue invitations by phone. Otherwise use your 'At Home' card, with the time of the party written under the word 'Cocktails'. You might write, for instance, 6 to 8 o'clock. This means two things to your guests, first, that no food will be served and, second, that they are expected to take their leave around 8 o'clock. In this way, they know exactly where they stand.

WHAT TO SERVE   What you serve is entirely up to you. It could be a sherry party, in which case you would serve two or three kinds of sherry or you can serve whisky, gin, champagne or indeed cocktails. Needless to say, it is far easier to stick to two or three kinds of drink than to offer all manner of combinations, unless you have a professional barman to cope. If you are catering mainly for businessmen, then whisky and gin are the obvious choice. In any event you should not fail to have one or two soft drinks also, since someone invariably calls for one.

Some people offer absolutely nothing else except a plate of crisps and nuts, but this *is* rather dreary, so do try to muster at least a few olives, some gherkins, cheese straws and similar nibblets which are served just as they are bought from the shop.

If you want to be a little more festive you will prepare, or buy, some canapés, perhaps a dish of tiny vol-au-vents filled with creamed shrimps or chicken, some tiny cheese tartlets, or two or three dishes of 'dips' into which guests can 'dunk' crisps or celery sticks. Even if you only have one hot hors d'oeuvre, or a steaming bowl of tiny cocktail sausages, it makes all the difference and adds that touch of indulgence which seems to go with parties. Do however cut your coat according to your cloth, for making canapés takes time, especially for large numbers. If you are having anything more than crisps do remember to have small paper napkins available, as your thoughtfulness will protect both your carpet and your guests' fingers.

HOW TO COPE   If you simply have a dozen friends dropping in for a drink, you have no problem. If you have more, then you will need to organize things a little more thoroughly and you will certainly need a barman-cum-waiter to dispense the drinks. In the case of your twelve friends your husband will serve the drinks and could indeed continue to act as barman, even if the guests were more than twelve, but for the fact that he will certainly want to be free to talk to his guests. This means that a hired barman is a 'must', unless, that is, you have a reliable male relative or even a close friend whom you could persuade to take on the task.

If you do have a friend dispensing the drinks, then you must certainly stick to a few limited choices, such as gin, whisky, sherry, or soft drink and you must further insist on his using a measure, otherwise, with the best will in the world, his inexperienced hand will betray him into despatching your liquor all too swiftly.

Whether professional or amateur you will need to agree with your barman how the drinks are to be served. He will either prepare a tray of mixed drinks at a table set up as a bar, then hand them around to the guests, or he will wait for guests to come up to the bar and order what they want. If the choice is limited, incidentally, it is far more sensible to say: 'We have whisky, gin or sherry. Which would you like?' The time-honoured phrase: 'What will you have?' does not really make sense unless a guest really has a complete choice. It is far too tempting to reply: 'What have you got?'

Having settled the matter of the barman-cum-waiter, you will need to decide whether you and your husband can cope on your own with taking coats from guests and showing the ladies where they can pretty up. If the answer is 'no', you will have to persuade another willing friend to help out, or even a teenage son or daughter. Failing this, you can of course hire another person from one of the agencies.

The question of cloakrooms also has to be settled in advance. The best arrangement is to have the men leave their coats in the hall, in the coat closet if there is one, while the women are shown to a room upstairs where they can leave their coats and make adjustments to their toilette before they make an entrance.

Once you have attended to these important details and the room is prepared with its flowers, the bar and side table tastefully laid out with dishes of nuts, canapés, dips and so on, you are ready to receive your first guests. If it is a small party you will introduce each new arrival to the others. If the party is a large one and most people have already arrived, then introduce new arrivals only to two or three people and let them take it from there. This also applies to latecomers. The whole party should not be brought to a halt to introduce them all around.

If you have no help, pass the tray of hors d'oeuvre around, then leave it on the previously prepared table so that guests can help themselves. Dips of course remain on the table all the time and guests are encouraged to help themselves. When everyone has arrived, slip into the kitchen and bring out your hot surprise, which you either hand around or invite people to come to the table for. This last procedure is quite a good one, since it breaks up groups and gets people mixing a little more.

Even if you have staff to help it is a good plan for you to go yourself for the hot snacks and bring them in with panache.

Otherwise your sole duty as a hostess is to move among your guests saying a few words to each one, reviving flagging conversations, bolstering up shy damsels, rescuing abandoned dowagers, deftly piloting a witty speaker out of the clutches of a notorious bore and generally enveloping everyone with warmth and friendliness. A simple enough matter.

The dinner party

Send out or telephone your invitations ten days to two weeks ahead of time and then get right down to your forward planning. Even before giving any detailed thought to the party you will have decided which kind it is to be, i.e. whether it will be entirely catered, whether you cook and hired help will serve, or whether you are to cope single-handed, with a little help from your man. If you are getting some help, make firm arrangements even before sending out the invitations, otherwise you may find that no one is available on that particular night.

MENU PLANNING   Your next task will be to plan the menu. It is not something to be done casually.

1 The first and unbreakable rule in menu planning is never to use your guests as guinea pigs. On no account should you

attempt a dish you have never made before, in your own interests as well in theirs.

2 As you weigh up the pro's and con's of this or that dish, remember that a meal, even if it is a dinner-party, must above all be substantial enough and well-balanced. If, for instance, you decide to begin with a consomme, then make sure your next dish is a good solid one. On the other hand, don't have a rich first course followed by an equally substantial second course and then a sickly dessert. As for providing a balanced meal, you know well enough what this means: you need to include protein, carbohydrate, fruit or vegetables, preferably both. The fact that it is a party is no reason to provide an unbalanced meal.

3 Take into account your guests' tastes. If, for instance, you have Jewish guests, do not serve pork. Bear in mind that while the English are not terribly keen on having a roast at a dinner party, people from abroad are anxious to have a typically English meal when invited into an English home and would be thrilled to be served roast beef and Yorkshire pudding. When entertaining guests you do not know well, it is sometimes better to ask discreetly whether there are any foods which do not agree with them. This is particularly advisable when entertaining your man's new boss and his lady.

4 Plan your menu to take advantage of foods which are in season. A first rate chef will always make his selection from vegetables and fruits which are in season and therefore at their best. This applies in spite of the prevalence of frozen food.

5 Think in terms of contrasts: different colours, textures, 'weight', bearing in mind that a meal needs eye-appeal. The mass-production technique has no place in menu planning. In other words, do not make the mistake of making pastry so

you can use it both for a main course and a dessert. If you do so you break two rules in one go: first of all you give your guests too much carbohydrate and secondly you short-change them on variety. So plan a varied meal.

6 Plan to have one 'exciting' dish to lift the meal into the party class. This special dish can be either the main course or a flamboyant dessert.

7 Finally, if you are going to be cook as well as hostess, bear in mind ease of preparation. There are various ways in which you can achieve this. One of them is to have a very simple first course which can be already on the table when your guests are seated. A simple first course does not mean a dreary one. Some very simple ideas are in fact quite festive. Avocado pear is a case in point. You can serve it simply with a tablespoon of vinaigrette in each cavity; with lemon juice ditto or scored with a silver knife and then filled with Madeira. Put back in the refrigerator when prepared and have one in each place as the guests file in. Another very simple yet festive first course is a slice of ripe melon draped with two or three slices of Parma ham. The only difficulty with this idea is that the ham has to be bought that very day and you can only contemplate it if the logistics are favourable.

Another easy first course to serve is soup, pre-prepared and only needing heating. In summer try iced vichyssoise or consommé Madrilène, both from your deep-freezer. If you serve consommé, iced or otherwise, do bear in mind that it is not very substantial and you will need to make up for this fact in the next course.

A casserole is perhaps the easiest main course to serve. You can even prepare it the day before and reheat it. You will lose nothing by taking this short cut. On the contrary, the taste of a casserole dish is usually better the second time around, as you no doubt are well aware. Other perfectly simple main courses are those concocted with escalope of veal, such as escalope of veal with Marsala or Madeira. They are more often than not served with peas, which are simple enough to prepare. You can then make a large pan of creamed potatoes, smooth down in the pan, trickle a thin layer of cream over the top and keep them in the oven until you are ready to serve them. At the moment of service, whisk in the cream *et voilà*.

As for the number of courses, three is just about right, especially if you are coping single-handed. There are no hard and fast rules, however, and if you feel like tossing in a fourth course, good for you.

SELECTING THE WINES Once you have planned your menu you will need to decide which wine, or wines, to serve with the meal. If your husband is an expert, he will probably take this whole question off your hands. If you are an expert too, then you're in for trouble! If both of you are greenhorns there are two courses open to you: (*a*) if you are willing and able to invest in a couple of bottles of good wine for the party, then get the advice of a reliable wine merchant, telling him what your main course is to be and what your wine budget is; (*b*) if you cannot run to anything fancy, then simply get a couple of bottles of *vin ordinaire* from the super-market or some Spanish Burgundy, an excellent buy, inci-dentally, and just put it on the table as it is.

THE TABLE The dinner party is of course the occasion for pulling out all the stops and putting to use your best silver, china dinner service, white damask table linen and so on. If you have these things, you would do well to get them pol-ished and spick and span well ahead of time. If you are not so blessed, do not worry, the cheaper modern pottery and gay place mats are great fun and there is just as much to be said for a cheerful up-to-the-minute table as there is for the more traditional trappings. So use what you have with ease and confidence and all will be well.

Lay your table as shown in Fig. 5, but using only the

cutlery and glasses which will actually be needed. In other words, if you are not serving fish, then omit the fish knives and forks and if there is to be only one wine, then obviously use only one glass. The bread-and-butter knife can be on the side plate if you prefer. Fish knives and forks are going out of fashion and it is nowadays perfectly in order to do without them.

Figure 5 A table setting

There should be enough salt, pepper and mustard pots to enable guests to serve themselves without too much to-ing and fro-ing: one set for every two guests is usually given as the right number, but if your dishes are properly seasoned, such a profusion of condiments on the table should be quite unnecessary. If you do not mind eating your meal through clouds of smoke, then have cigarettes in small containers and ashtrays here and there on the table. If you prefer to taste your food, then you have every right to omit this barbarous 'refinement' and bring on the cigarettes with the coffee, or better still, offer them later in the living-room.

If you and your husband have no help, then he will serve the wine and the bottle should be conveniently placed at the head of the table. If it is an expensive old wine you will serve it lovingly in a wine basket, but do not make a laughing stock of yourself by placing a bottle of 'plonk' in a basket or decanting it into a cut glass decanter. Just put it on the table. If you are having champagne, which incidentally complements every dish, you will need to have it in a bucket of ice on a small table near the head of the table, with a table napkin nearby. Your husband can then take out the bottle, wrap the napkin around its neck, open it and serve the champagne. Do not try it, however, unless your husband can carry out these operations skilfully, for nothing looks clumsier than a man struggling ineptly with a bottle of champagne.

Finally, you will need flowers to finish off your table. Get something that will last and have your arrangements finished the day before the party. Make it a low arrangement so that it does not prevent your guests from seeing their vis-à-vis. Choose colours to complement the colour scheme and do not go for anything too highly perfumed, as this is distracting during a meal. If you are planning to have candles, make sure that you are well supplied and that holders are in perfect condition. Candles are especially appropriate for evening parties, but should not be the only source of lighting in the room. If your dinner party is to have strong business overtones, however, you would be well advised not to have candles. One of those low-slung lights hanging close to the table are far better for business talk, as men like to see what they're doing and like to look their opponent in the eye.

As you lay your table get the seating arrangement set in your mind, so that when your guests arrive both you and your husband already know where to seat them. For purely social occasions it is customary to separate husbands and wives and to alternate the seating between men and women so that every man has a woman on either side of him and vice versa. The host takes the head of the table and the hostess the foot. The most important woman guest is seated at the host's right, the most important male guest to the hostess's right. The second most important woman guest sits on the host's left and the second most important male guest sits on the hostess's left.

As a businessman's wife, however, you will frequently be entertaining a party containing more men than women and indeed on some occasions you may even be the only woman. Moreover your husband will quite frequently have his own reasons for wanting Joe Bloggs on his right and John Doakes on his left. So ask him what his preferences are as to seating and, other things being equal, spread the girls out evenly all around the table like rare spices. If the party is a large one do not hesitate to have place cards, then you will be sure that no last minute scuffles will take place when guests go into the dining-room.

If you are entertaining a clutch of big-wigs, then the question of precedence enters into the matter of seating arrangements and it is surprising how much importance some people attach to such minutiae. So if in doubt, and who isn't—consult *Whitaker's Almanack*. The Lord Lieutenant of the County deals with such inquiries with regard to county dignitaries, while the Marshal of the Diplomatic Corps at the Foreign Office can help you if foreign diplomats are involved. If you are entertaining local authority personnel, the Town Clerk, Lord Mayor or Mayor's office, the local squire, vicar or editor of the local paper are useful sources of information.

On the day

What happens on the day will depend, once again, on what staff you have to help you. Regardless of whether you did all the cooking yourself or had the whole meal brought in by outside caterers, there are three possibilities on the day: you have one helper in the kitchen and another to serve, you have one helper only or you have no help at all.

If you have hired a maid or a manservant to serve the meal, he or she will open the door, relieve the guests of their coats and usher them to the living-room, where you will be waiting for them. If you are without help, you and your husband will share these duties between you, then he will serve the sherry or cocktails, while you hand around olives, nuts or what have you. If there is a maid, she can do this, while you slip into the kitchen and attend to any last minute preparations.

When dinner is ready, simply say to your guests: 'Shall we go in to dinner now?' The first course should already be on the table. Your husband will pour the wine, unless there is a manservant. When the first course is over the hired help clears the plates, then proceeds in one of two ways: (1) if the host is serving the main course, places a pile of warm plates in front of him and brings him the casserole or what have you ready to serve. The host then fills each plate, the maid picks it up and places it in front of each guest, beginning with the lady on the host's right and proceeding anti-clockwise until she gets back to the host, whom she serves last. (2) if the meal is being dished up in the kitchen by Little Helper No. 2, then the maid brings in the dishes and presents them to each guest in turn. She can present the meat dish in one hand and the vegetables in the other. If you have settled for this mode of serving, then the maid will have previously put a warm plate before each guest.

If you are on your own, then there will be nothing for it but for you to clear away the plates and produce warm plates and the main dish, which you will place before your husband for service. The same will happen with the dessert, except that you will serve it yourself and, if you are wise, you will have it all ready on the sideboard in individual containers.

When the meal is over, you will say: 'Shall we move over to the living-room for our coffee?' At this point you can show the women where to brush up if necessary, then disappear into the kitchen to get the coffee. Some nice husbands take care of the coffee themselves to allow their wife to spend a little more time with her guests. Of course, if you have some help, you will not have this problem. If you prefer, you can serve the coffee right at the dinner table, but it is far more comfortable to move on to the living-room and this has the additional advantage of enabling everyone to 'pay a call' en route.

Needless to say, if you are serving brandy or port, now is the time to do it and by now too you have no choice but to permit the air to be polluted with smoke.

Buffet parties

Buffet parties are supposed to be a way of entertaining a large number of people with less wear and tear on the hostess. Do not be deceived, however, for even if the serving is eliminated, the cooking, preparing and clearing up are not. Since the people to be fed are more, it follows that the buffet party is not less work. Perhaps its complete lack of formality makes it seem less stressful and, in any case it has its uses, especially at holiday times.

Ideally you should serve only food which can be eaten with a fork alone, unless you are having small tables at which guests can sit. A casserole or chafing-dish meal would be ideal. All other food should be cold and easy to eat. The dessert could be a large bowl of fruit salad with a jug of cream nearby.

Arrange your table tastefully, with the plates in piles, the table napkins and cutlery all lined up ready to be picked up and the foods conveniently located so that guests can help themselves without difficulty. Place the table so that guests can move all the way around it, especially if the number of guests is large.

The wine and glasses will be on the table too and your husband can pour the first glass as each guest comes up to the table and let them help themselves to refills.

You might have the cold dishes on the table when the guests arrive and then bring in the hot dish at the appropriate moment. Clear away dirty plates and filled ashtrays promptly. After the dessert, bring in the coffee and leave it on the table so that guests can serve themselves. Don't omit to invite them to do so, however, as some guests are quite shy, even in this day and age.

Unexpected guests

What separates the perfect hostess from the run-of-the-mill variety, we are told, is the ability to rustle up an impromptu meal for an unexpected guest. Such a feat is not really so hard to accomplish, providing you insist on getting at least *some* notice and that you think in term of a meal or a snack, but not a festive meal. The feeling should be that you are simply adding an extra place or two at the family table and you too should try to think of it in this way. Having rid yourself of the idea that you ought to provide a banquet, you might try coping with unexpected guests by:

1 *Making use of a deep-freeze* Large joints and birds of course take too long to defrost to be of any help, but chops, steaks and above all escalopes of veal are ideal for last minute cooking. An escalope will defrost in about half an hour and enable you to produce, for instance, escalopes with Marsala in next to no time. Add peas and creamed potatoes and your main course is very elegantly taken care of. Not only vegetables and ice cream will go in the deep-freeze, but even finished dishes only needing warming up.

2 *Cook in batches* If you do this you will be able to rustle up a meal without even a last-minute rush to the shops. You could lay aside a day for cooking and prepare: (*a*) enough pastry to last you a week (just put it in a floured cloth and park it in the refrigerator); (*b*) a bottle of vinaigrette (just shake and use when needed); (*c*) a roll of maître d'hôtel butter (just cut off a medallion of it and place on each grilled steak); (*d*) a jar of apricot glaze to use on flans, tartlets, etc.; (*e*) a tin of meringues from which to make instant desserts; (*f*) a jar of basic sauce, which keeps almost indefinitely and has a hundred uses. One could go on almost indefinitely, but

you get the idea. Other things, such as bottling surplus fruit you can do when the occasion arises rather than on a fixed date.

3 *Institute the old-fashioned stock pot habit* There is really nothing old-fashioned about a stock pot. No self-respecting chef would operate without one. It gives you an instant soup, in one of two ways: (*a*) add a handful of *pastina*, which you can buy at most Continental grocers'; or (*b*) have the right quantity of stock boiling rapidly, then toss in a raw egg. Beat vigorously as you do so and serve. Always have a dish of grated Parmesan cheese on the table for each guest to sprinkle on to taste. But of course this isn't all a stock pot will do for you: it will enrichen your casseroles and form the basis for gravies, add richness to tinned soups if used in place of water; permit you to rustle up a risotto in half an hour. If you happen to have some chicken livers in the deep-freeze, fry them lightly in butter, add tomato paste, a little red wine and some of that stock, sit them in a bed of the risotto and your whole meal is made. No need for any first course, just a little fresh fruit to end the meal.

4 Always have a good stock of staples in the house. Apart from the more obvious things, have the *pastina*, already mentioned, noodles, Patna rice, *pasta reale*, which tossed on a steaming bowl of tomato soup (canned) lifts it into another class; tomato purée, small tins of pâté de foie gras, plenty of cheese, of course, a tinned boned ham, which heated and coated with a Madeira sauce can make a meal in itself and always plenty of fruit and lettuce, radishes, celery and so on. Many more similar ideas will occur to you.

It is only fair to add that many a valiant businessman's wife copes admirably with any number of unexpected guests without resorting to either (1), (2) or (3). Upon hearing the glad tidings that a guest or two is about to descend upon them, she scurries over to the shops, buys the needful and dashes back to prepare a delectable meal. It seems to be a question of where there's a will there's a way.

Visitors from abroad

Some hostesses are rather put out at the idea of entertaining someone from abroad. They worry in case their cooking will be found unacceptable; they wonder whether they will be able to understand each other; they fret about foreign customs and heavens knows what. There really is no need for any of this. The first thing to bear in mind is that we are all alike under the skin. If anything strikes you as strange about someone who does not speak your language, remember that the strangeness is only superficial. Below the surface you are as one. This thought really sums it up.

Secondly, anyone visiting Britain from abroad, whether on business or pleasure-bent, is delighted to be received into an English home and is not about to criticise you or make you feel uncomfortable.

In the third place bear in mind that receiving a foreign visitor is easier than being received abroad, for the visitor is the one who is supposed to conform to the customs he finds abroad. You must therefore confidently carry on with your usual practices and let the guest follow you.

This said, the thoughtful hostess will naturally want to do what she can to make her overseas guest comfortable and not give him any food which goes against his religion or is apt to be unpleasant to him. As already mentioned, most overseas visitors like to have English food when in England and nothing could please them more, therefore, if you present them with roast beef and Yorkshire pudding, especially since it is so hard to come by in restaurants these days. It would be a mistake for you to attempt to serve Italian food to an Italian, German food to a German and Chinese food to a Chinese. So stick to your usual repertoire, but if you are entertaining Muslims, Jews or anyone extremely exotic ask your man to find out what foods they may not eat and always have non-alcoholic beverages available.

Bear in mind that Latins do not care for stodgy puddings or dumplings and do not care for mint sauce or redcurrant jelly. Central Europeans, on the other hand, may well appreciate these very things. Many Americans do not like high meals, rabbit or such things as kidneys, brain or sweetbread, but these are, of course, generalizations and you must not worry about likes and dislikes unduly.

Some people from other countries find our English table manners a little daunting and hard to live up to. So keep a furtive eye on your foreign guests and if you see any sign of an unequal struggle taking place between a diner, armed with knife and fork, and a chicken, for instance, promptly brandish your own drum stick with your fingers and say: 'Use your fingers it's easier', or just urge them on with a smile if you cannot set the example.

And finally, if your foreign guests do something you do not like, try to refrain from labelling them ill-mannered. They may just be doing what everyone does in their own country.

A Business of Your Own

LESLEY BERNSTEIN AND SYLVIA PASKIN

Every day thousands of people dream about setting up a business of their own. The attractions of independence, of being 'your own boss', are strong. Many eventually take that step and never regret it. Here are true stories of people who have set up on their own – what made them take that step, their problems, their successes, their methods and mistakes. Written by two professional journalists, this is an excellent way of seeing how to do it, by reading how others have 'made the break'.

A PAPERBACK ORIGINAL
7½″×4½″ (191×114 mm)   112 pp

ISBN 0 220 66832 9   **50p**

How to Get a Better Job in Management

IAN MACHORTON

Gold watches for twenty-five years of service are being given far less frequently these days, as job mobility is increasingly becoming an accepted aspect of working life, especially among managerial levels. Unfortunately, this mobility is not always voluntary, and the redundant middle or senior manager is becoming an anxious yet familiar figure in the seventies. This immensely valuable book, written by an author who has trained and advised thousands in their search for new careers, shows how to go about getting that vital next job. There is a special section for people leaving the services and looking for a second career.

A PAPERBACK ORIGINAL
7½″×4½″ (191×114 mm)   112 pp
ISBN 0 220 66830 2

50p

Simon Elliott's Quick Guides to Letter-Writing

SIMON ELLIOTT

Simon Elliott is a distinguished lawyer and Member of Parliament, writing under a pseudonym. A skilled correspondent, Mr. Elliott averages at least thirty letters a day. In this book, he puts his experience and expertise at the service of his readers. Whether you seek success in a business or profession – or merely the satisfaction of expressing your thoughts to your friends, in a clear, concise and admirable style – these Guides should serve you well.

A PAPERBACK ORIGINAL

$7\frac{1}{2}'' \times 4\frac{1}{2}''$ (191 × 114 mm)   112 pp

ISBN 0 220 66833 7   **50p**

Simon Elliott's Quick Guides to Speaking in Public

SIMON ELLIOTT

From best man to company chairman, from a farewell party to a television interview – hardly anyone escapes having to speak to a gathering of people a few times in their lives. And the more successful a person is in his career or hobby, the more he has to speak in public. This book is written by a person (Simon Elliott is his pen name) who is much sought after as an after dinner speaker, who has been successfully speaking in public since school debates, and through courts and parliament. His book is an excellent guide to what to say, when to say it, and how to say it.

A PAPERBACK ORIGINAL

$7\frac{1}{2}'' \times 4\frac{1}{2}''$ (191×114 mm)   112 pp

ISBN 0 220 66831 0

50p

Some titles published in hardback by Business Books Limited

No. of copies	International standard book number	price	title
....	0 220 66875 2	£3·50	**The businessman's guide to letter-writing and to the law on letters** *Mitchell*
....	0 220 99252 5	£5·25	**The businessman's guide to travel and to profits abroad** *Mitchell*
....	0 220 66868 x	£2·75	**Buying and running your own business** *Ford*
....	0 220 66799 3	£3·75	**Enjoying a profitable business** *Hazel & Reid*
....	0 220 69859 7	£2·25	**Etiquette for the businessman** *Bosticco*
,,,,,,,,,,	0 220 79891 5	£3·50	**Finance for the non-accountant** *Rockley*
....	0 220 79865 6	£3·25	**Fund raising techniques** *Phillips*
....	0 220 66815 9	£4·50	**Goodwill – the wasted asset** *Biddlecombe*
....	0 220 79419 7	£4·75	**Graphics ad lib** *Hinwood*
....	0 220 79866 4	£2·75	**Industrial intelligence and espionage** *Slee Smith*
....	0 220 66816 7	£2·75	**The myth of the computer** *Rothery*
....	0 220 99222 3	£3·25	**Spending advertising money** *Broadbent*
....	0 220 99261 4	£4·75	**Successful project management** *Taylor & Watling*
....	0 220 66851 5	£2·75	**Survival by competence** *Rothery*

ORDER FROM YOUR BOOKSELLER
Simply mark the books you require on this form and give it to your normal bookseller

All enquiries to:
BUSINESS BOOKS LIMITED, Mercury House, Waterloo Road, London SE1 8UL Telephone: 01-928 3388

Customer's Name and Address

Date: Order No.